HISTORICALLY BLACK GUIDE TO WEALTH

FINANCIAL LIBERTY FOR AFRICAN AMERICANS

KEVIN M. LEWIS

authorHOUSE®

AuthorHouse™
1663 Liberty Drive
Bloomington, IN 47403
www.authorhouse.com
Phone: 833-262-8899

This book is a work of non-fiction. Unless otherwise noted, the author and the publisher make no explicit guarantees as to the accuracy of the information contained in this book and in some cases, names of people and places have been altered to protect their privacy.

Published by AuthorHouse 08/26/2021

ISBN: 978-1-6655-3592-2 (sc)
ISBN: 978-1-6655-3594-6 (e)

Print information available on the last page.

Any people depicted in stock imagery provided by Getty Images are models, and such images are being used for illustrative purposes only.
Certain stock imagery © Getty Images.

This book is printed on acid-free paper.

Because of the dynamic nature of the Internet, any web addresses or links contained in this book may have changed since publication and may no longer be valid. The views expressed in this work are solely those of the author and do not necessarily reflect the views of the publisher, and the publisher hereby disclaims any responsibility for them.

CONTENTS

INTRODUCTION

Ugh, money? Again the topic of conversation, Marlon thinks. *Can't I just get a stack of tickets and win the lottery?* Well, no Marlon. You can't because the odds of that happening are 1 in 302,575,350. In other words, you have a greater chance of getting struck by lightning forty-two times in your life. If you did get struck by lightning, at least your money obstacles go away. Unless, of course, you survive.

Marlon is a thirty-eight-year-old black man who graduated from one of the top Historically Black Colleges and Universities (HBCUs) in the nation. He has a decent-paying job, a good financial support system, and no major health or personal complications that would prevent him from enjoying a beautiful life. He is living paycheck to paycheck with no more than $400 in the bank for emergencies. He has a FICO score of 608, he's never heard of business credit, and he has no real assets or wealth to talk about, let alone pass on to his two beautiful daughters. He doesn't even have health or life insurance, which means if something were to happen to him, those daughters would inherit only his student loan bills and whatever health or mortality debt that came along if he did, in fact, get struck by lightning.

I was Marlon, although the name was changed to protect the ignorant. The good news for me is that I survived that time in my life and am now fifty. What I understand much more fully now is how budgets, credit, assets, and asset acquisition work together to create the life that few people have but most people dream of. I want to do everything in my power to help the next twenty-, thirty-, or forty-year-old understand these concepts, so they don't have to wait until they are fifty to start enjoying life. I decided to put this book together to help the 99 percent understand what the 1 percent have known and used for years.

We are constantly exposed to people such as Jeff Bezos who can get divorced, give his wife $35 billion dollars in the settlement, and still be the wealthiest person in America. These people tell us that we can have the same level of success just as easily. They make us feel inadequate if we don't achieve it by working our way to the top. What they don't mention is many of them have parents, relatives, friends, and associates who gave them a financial boost to get them going. Now I don't know about you, but I can't just call up my uncle and ask to borrow $75,000 really quick, and I'll pay him back when my business "blows up."

In our culture, we are often reminded that there is an American Dream. But there are those of us who aren't sure what it is or how to get there, so it remains just that—a dream. This book is for you. It is written for people who see millionaires and billionaires continually displaying the power and lifestyles that financial liberty provides and who are left wondering how that liberty manages to be passed on from generation to generation. The American Dream is not the same for all of us. In fact, not only is the dream different for each person, but my brothers and sisters are not all equipped with the same tools that others might be. Some of you want material wealth, some of you may want to use finances to move into the political arena, and some of you wish to set up a better life for your children, whatever your dream, financial liberty is likely to be a crucial step in achieving it.

People often spend a great deal of time reading books and other publications, following blogs, or listening to podcasts that discuss the latest, greatest, low-effort way to achieve financial freedom. Some of those sources contain advice based on sound principles that can work for anyone. Others may be just a way to sell the book or enroll people in seminars. Very few of the sources address the unique financial challenges that minorities are likely to face as they set out to build and pass on wealth—particularly African Americans, who started out behind in this country and seldom have the same advantages afforded their white peers.

I recall reading *Rich Dad Poor Dad*, by Robert Kiyosaki, which had a profound effect on my life. It taught me the difference between having a healthy relationship with money and an unhealthy one. What I later realized about that book is that Kiyosaki did not actually have a "poor" dad. He comes from a two-parent household, and both his parents had middle-class jobs. He also had a rich "dad"—his friend's father—who built a successful business. The exposure to these two things alone gave him an advantage that I and most of my friends didn't have the luxury of experiencing. Please don't get me wrong. It's a great book, and I recommend it to everyone who wants to learn how wealth works. But it does not represent my reality. I grew up in a single-parent household, and even though we were upper-middle-class—thanks to a mother who did very well for herself in corporate America—I don't think any of my relatives could have given me $25K at one time without having to eat ramen noodles for a year as a sacrifice. My friends certainly didn't have wealthy parents or relatives. I know that because most of my friends came over to my house to live out their *Lifestyles of the Rich and Famous* dreams.

I'm here to help you because I've been there before. I understand how irritatingly exhausting it is to waste money and time utilizing resources with methods that don't apply to you. This book was made to address wealth in a way that uses *your* story, or a story that may be more familiar to you than that of Elon Musk. Your dilemmas are not the same as those of the majority. This book uses tactics to combat our specific obstacles to build a better, more financially liberal black America.

This book uses a system for wealth-building called the Four Pillars of Financial Liberty™ (4PFL™). The pillars are:

- Budgeting strategy
- Personal credit
- Business credit
- Asset acquisition

4PLF is a method of establishing a solid foundation for building wealth for those who don't have many resources to begin with. Each pillar can be customized according to your financial situation, but all are necessary for building *true wealth*—an economic survival requirement of the society we live in.

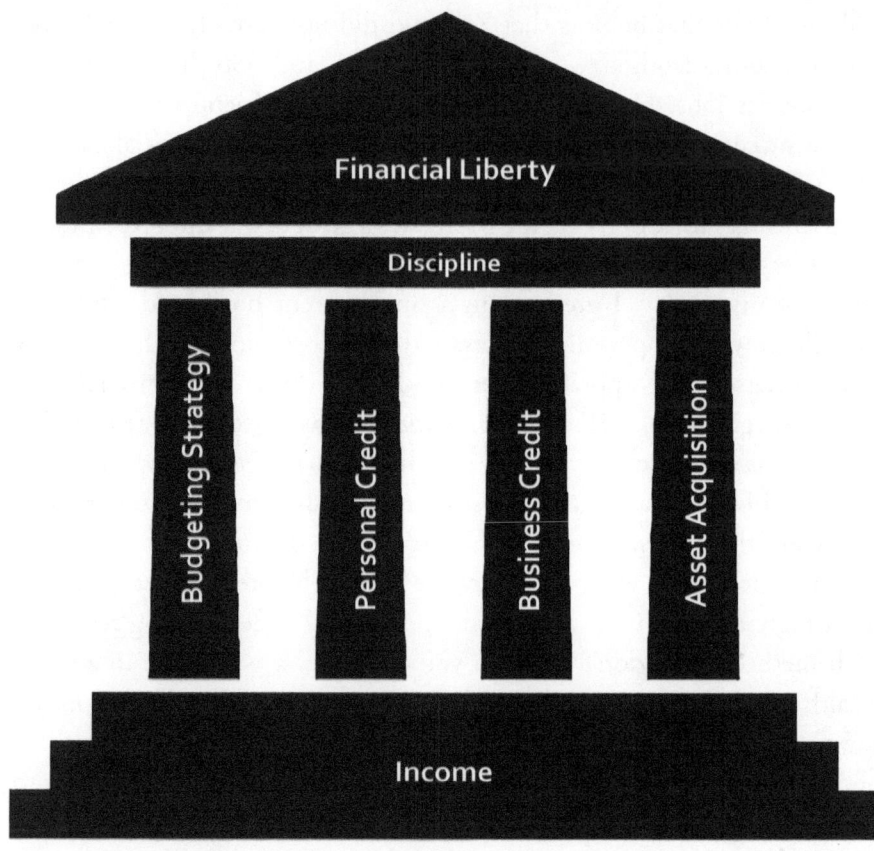

Fig. 1   The Four Pillars of Financial Liberty

So how did 4PFL™ come to be? As I mentioned before, many books, articles, website blogs, and social media posts have been written about wealth building. Many of the principles, guidelines, techniques, and tools are accurate and effective, but I have found that they commonly assume you have access to substantial resources. Credible sources all say that resources—whether financial, personal, or professional—are necessary as a starting point. How many times have you heard someone say, "Your network determines your net worth"? While there is no debate that having networks gives you many advantages, the biggest challenge in most black communities is that not many people have access to great networks. Take Philadelphia as an example. Chestnut Hill is the wealthiest neighborhood in Philadelphia with a median household income of a cool $100,099 per year. Now compare that to Fairhill, the poorest neighborhood in the city, with a dismal $18,722 median income. Can you guess the racial makeup of Chestnut Hill? It's 70.61 percent white, 17.57 percent black and Latino, 5.6 percent Asian, and 6.22 percent mixed or classified as "other." Can you guess the racial makeup of Fairhill? It's 37.07 white, 58.31 percent black and Latino, 0.32 percent Asian, and 4.3 percent mixed or identified as "other." Figure 2 shows some even more staggering statistics regarding wealth in America.

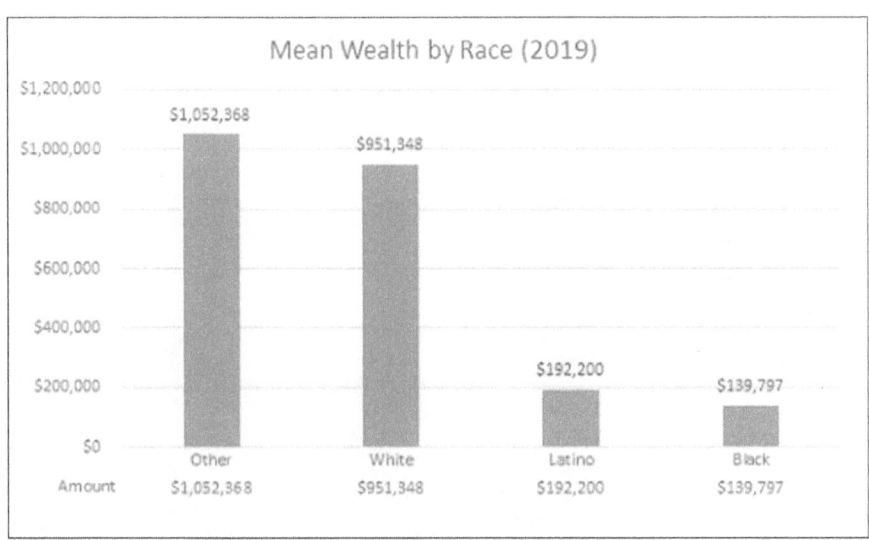

Fig. 2 Income According to Race

Has anyone ever had the audacity to tell you, "If you hang with nine broke friends, you're bound to be the tenth one"? The problem with that advice is that 10 percent of the world's population holds 90 percent of the world's wealth. In other words, among ten people chosen at random from the world's population, only one of those people is likely to hold significant wealth. In our Philadelphia example, black people are more likely to be hanging around nine broke friends than rich friends, so it makes sense that their net worth is going to be low because their network has low incomes. So please excuse us if we're not hanging always around Jay-Z and Beyoncé for the sake of our income.

I am an adjunct professor at a Cheyney University, where I had an entrepreneurship class of forty-seven adult students ranging in age from thirty-four to fifty-nine. I asked them to raise their hands if they knew someone whose net worth was $1 million or more. I wasn't surprised when not one person's hand went up. I then asked them to raise their hands if they knew someone whose net worth was $500K or more. Still no hands. Only when the figure dropped to $200K did two people in the group raise their hands. Most of the group couldn't name a person whose net worth was more than $30K. Some of the group even struggled with the term "net worth." It was in this moment that something sparked in me: I couldn't let this be the future of this generation or the next. It prompted me to do something, and that day in class is substantially the inspiration of what you now hold in your hands—a guide toward building black wealth.

PART 1

FOUNDATION

After many of my students struggled with the term "net worth," I realized the importance of distinguishing between income and net worth. I also realized that most of my friends don't know the difference either, and understanding those differences plays a significant role in wealth building.

What Is Income?

There are two types of income:

Earned income is money made by an individual and directly tied to that person's efforts. If the individual does not put forth the effort, there is no earned income. For example, if a tax accountant does not prepare taxes for her clients because she is on vacation, she will not have any earned income.

Passive income is money that is made by an individual without being directly tied to his or her efforts. For example, if a tax accountant has people working for her who prepare taxes for her clients, the percentage of money she takes from their efforts is called passive income. She could be on vacation, and if they are working while she is away, she is receiving passive income.

What Is Net Worth?

Net worth can be expressed by the following equation:

Assets − Liabilities = Net Worth

Asset: Anything that has value greater than the cost to maintain it. Example: Shante has a car with a payment of $300/month; insurance of $200/month; and maintenance, tolls, and fuel of $500/month. Total cost to maintain that car is $1,000. If Shante uses that car to drive for Uber and makes $1,500/month doing so then she has an asset worth $500 per month.

Fig. 3 Examples of Assets

Liability: Anything that has value less than the cost to maintain it. Example: Shante has a car with a payment of $300/month; insurance of $200/month; and maintenance, tolls, and fuel of $500/month. Total cost to maintain that car is $1,000. If Shante uses that car to drive for Uber and makes $900/month doing so, then she has a liability of $100 per month.

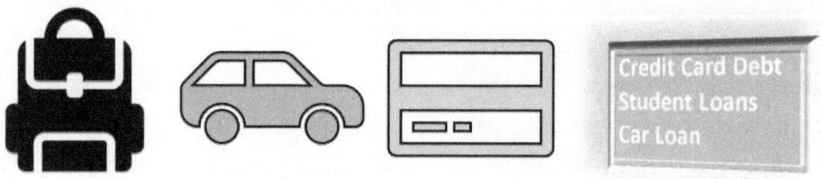

Fig. 4 Examples of Liabilities

If you add the value of all your assets and subtract the cost of all your liabilities, you get your net worth. Income is what you earn; net worth is what is earned for you.

There are a few issues with net worth. The first, and probably most important, is that it is not a topic of conversation among that 90 percent of whom I spoke about earlier. Most people talk about income instead of net worth. In other words, we talk about how much we make per year and view that as our measuring stick. If Darryl makes $100K/year and has $25K in his savings account, he may be considered rich or wealthy by some standards. That demonstrates a consumer mentality and is part of the reason there aren't very many wealthy people in the world generally, and in the United States specifically.

Wealthy people talk about acquiring assets, while the rest talk about increasing income when discussing their value. The difference is not about income but the *mindset* it takes to manage it. The problem is people make enough money to wear Louis Vuitton boots and scarves and call themselves rich. If you have something to show for it, that's all that matters, right? Wrong. This is the poor mindset that we may find ourselves subject to. It creates a cycle that hinders us from building a legacy for our children. Now I am not implying that anyone who isn't in the top 10 percent is in poverty. Poverty is a number that is determined by the US Department of Labor, so those of you who do make $100k a year, you can unclench your jaw and butt cheeks. I'm not calling you broke, I am simply distinguishing mindsets, not income.

The second problem with net worth is with how people often misunderstand assets. Many people view houses as assets. But your house is *not* an asset if you have a mortgage on it. Even if you pay the mortgage off, it still isn't a true asset. Unless the money you generate from the property is greater than the property tax, utility bills, maintenance, and a host of other expenses, it is still considered a liability. It doesn't become an actual asset until you sell it for more than you paid in all those expenses over time, or when you rent it for more than the monthly expenses you incur. Understanding assets thoroughly and accurately is necessary for building true wealth.

Many types of assets exist in the world today. Real estate is probably the most reliable because it has outperformed all other assets over time. In other words, you get the highest returns on your investments in real estate. However, acquiring real estate is not as simple and accessible to some individuals as other assets are. One of the biggest challenges to acquiring real estate is *money*. The African American community has much less access to money and other capital than other ethnicities in this country, which is why we own much less real estate than any other ethnicity.

As I said, real estate is just one of many potential assets but there are plenty of others. Let's take Jordan's for example. How do you turn a pair of Js into an asset? Well, if you bought them for $150, you'd have to sell them for $200 and buy another pair until the profit you have made (three pairs of sneakers) allows you to pay for the pair you wanted to wear. Understanding how to turn income into assets is the true key to increasing your net worth. We discuss this in detail when we talk about the fourth pillar.

Another barrier of building wealth that happens among the African American population is education. If you look up statistics for people who have won the lottery, for example, you will find that an overwhelming number of them end up financially worse off than they did before they won the money. So how does a person who has won $5M go broke? The answers lie in a number of factors. A small percentage of it relates to addictive behaviors like gambling and drug or alcohol abuse, those things that are most often highlighted in the media. But it is more likely to have been a direct result of a lack of financial knowledge. There is an old saying: "Money doesn't make you who you are, it only amplifies who you are." So, if a person makes $30K/year and spends all of the money on alcohol and drugs, there is a strong possibility that when he or she gets $30M, the individual will spend all of it on alcohol and drugs as well. In addition to that, it is not unusual for someone who plays the lottery regularly and wins small amounts of money to become addicted to the excitement of winning and plows his or her million-dollar winnings into more lottery tickets until all the money is gone.

However, it is more often the case that if you go from living check-to-check to being a millionaire, your concept of the buying power of a million dollars is limited. Chances are you'll start spending without putting into perspective the ongoing costs that your new million-dollar house may have. It's like when your kids tell you that $100 is a lot of money, and you look at them in a comical and adorable manner but really you're thinking, *wait 'til you get some bills*. Well, millionaires look at naive lottery winners the same way, believe it or not. "Aww he just bought a $2M dollar house with the $5M he just won. Wait 'til he gets the electric bill, the lawn care, the pool service, and so on."

One of the reasons wealthy people say if you want to be a millionaire you should surround yourself with millionaires is that they are already millionaires, and they are making money telling other people how to how to keep or grow their millions. Take the children of rich celebrities for example. They grow up in an environment that constantly exposes them to knowledge about how to make money. While they are often portrayed in the media as a bit impulsive at times, their free financial education has afforded them the ability to make money even when they are not trying. They are able to leverage their family status into lucrative reality shows and sitcoms and guest appearances in nightclubs, retail stores, and shopping malls all around the world. People actually pay them to do nothing but be themselves. This might not be possible if they hadn't had a financial education as a young person. On the other hand, if they had been surrounded by alcoholics and drug addicts, there is a great likelihood that they would have ended up as addicts or alcoholics as well. Of course, there are plenty of instances where people have made it out of difficult circumstances and became wealthy. Take, for instance, Jay-Z, the first hip-hop billionaire. He overcame seemingly insurmountable odds to get to his position in life. But he is not typical. So, it is difficult to disagree with the statement that "The greater your resources the greater your financial potential."

One of the other predicaments we encounter regarding finance is the "get-rich-quick" mentality. How many of us have bought a book, seen an advertisement, been to a seminar, or gotten an invitation from someone that says you can get rich in ninety days or fewer? We have all probably been exposed to a multilevel marketing opportunity whereby a host brings you in a room, tells you he or she became a millionaire in just six months. The individual tells you that he or she had an excellent job making decent money, but just wasn't fulfilled. The person goes on to tell you how he or she only works ten hours per week, and you could do the same if you just followed the individual's proven system of success. The person will show you a product or service, tell you that the product or service is the best in the industry, that it is endorsed by some celebrity, and you can get in on the opportunity for a small fee. According to this individual, you are special because you get to learn the "business" from the person who started it, and it is a privilege to just be in the room with him or her. "How many of you get to spend one hour every week with the CEO of the company you work for?" the individual will ask. Then the person will strongly suggest that you spend the $497 to go to a two-day seminar, so you can learn how he or she achieved such phenomenal success. And at this two-day seminar, the individual will suggest that you purchase all the marketing materials, and because you came this time, you can get them at deep discounts. It will then be strongly suggested that you register for the next seminar. What you're not told is that you may end up paying $497 for the seminar, $300 for the flight to get there, $200 for the rental car, $200 for the hotel, $200 for the materials, and $200 for food and entertainment. At the end of the weekend, you have spent $1,597 for this "opportunity," and the individual wants you to do that repeatedly several more times throughout the year. For many of us, $1,597 is all we have saved or is the only money we will have all year to buy the things we want. You are then told that to obtain wealth, you must make sacrifices, and it is passively suggested that you borrow the money to get to the seminar. Now you realize that all this may have been a scam, and who got rich? The person at the top. He or she is absolutely correct in saying that in order to obtain wealth you must make sacrifices, but at some point, you have to decide what is most feasible for you.

I am not condemning all multilevel marketing organizations outright. Nor am I saying they don't work sometimes. Mary Kay, Avon, and Primerica have created wealth for many of their consultants. Experience shows that the people who typically do well in these companies are those who either have a spouse who can support them financially while they learn how to build their businesses, or they have some money coming in from another source that can offset the investment in money and time it takes to build the business. Again, in no way am I saying all of them are schemes and scams and that no one out there is making money. Simply put, many of us do not have access to the resources we need to be successful with these types of opportunities. More realistically, to build wealth, we need to be able to tap into the limited resources we have and develop a system for turning *those* resources into steady, consistent, and tangible growth. This book explains how to get to that position of financial liberty by utilizing the resources that most of us have at our disposal. This is where the Four Pillars of Financial Liberty™ comes in.

Income Preservation

The Four Pillars of Financial Liberty™ (4PFL) is like building a house. As with all buildings, we want to start by laying a solid foundation and set the pillars on top. Figure 5 shows the four pillars standing on a solid slab called "Income," which in finance is just as important as the pillars themselves. Generating income is a simple concept, but many people take it for granted and don't recognize how critical it is to protect all the elements that help you keep the income flowing.

To demonstrate the impact of income, I'll use Darryl as an example. Darryl is a twenty-nine-year-old man living in Richmond, Virginia. He has a college degree in social work from Virginia Union University. Darryl drives a 2012 Honda Accord that was given to him by his aunt, and it is in fairly decent shape. Darryl lives alone in a one-bedroom apartment and pays $635 per month in rent. Although he applied for many jobs in the social work field, he had to take a job as a case manager with a home health care agency to pay his bills. That job pays him $31K per year, and he brings home roughly $2K per month after taxes. Following is a list of Darryl's monthly expenses:

Rent—$635
Utilities—$160
Cable—$110
Groceries—$250
Car Insurance—$135
Miscellaneous—$200
Total—$1,490

As you can see, he will have approximately $500 left after he pays these expenses. The good news about Darryl is that he is pretty thrifty when it comes to buying clothes, and he rarely spends more than he budgets for when he is shopping. However, he does like to go out to clubs on the weekends and often spends $75–$100 on food, travel, and entertainment. As you can see, he runs a tight budget with little to spare.

One day while Darryl is on his way to work, his car's timing belt breaks, and his mechanic quotes him $479 to fix it. In addition, he says he needs new rotors and calipers, which will be an additional $312 to fix. In total, his car is going to cost him $791 in repairs. Darryl's job is a forty-two-minute drive from his home and using public transportation to get there is extremely difficult. So having his car is essential for getting to work. Darryl doesn't have many days left to take off from work because he has already taken off thirteen days. Some of his time was used for pleasure, but some was used for minor occurrences that required his time away.

At this point you may be thinking, *what does any of this have to do with the income foundation?* Let's look at how two components above may affect Darryl. He is going to have to take off at least one day from work to get his car repaired. Because Darryl didn't plan for that time off, he risks losing his job for using too much time away. Had he considered this a possibility before he took those two days off in June because it was a nice day and he just didn't feel like going to work, he would have more liberty to take off the days. If Darryl takes the day off to get the car fixed and loses his job because of it, he is going to have to dip into whatever savings he has to keep himself afloat until he gets another job, or he's going to have to use some kind of credit or borrow the money from friends or family to finance his life. This could affect his future finances or his relationships.

In addition, Darryl did not plan on this $791 expense. Now he has to figure out where the money is going to come from. Had he included a monthly car maintenance expense in his budget, he might be able to respond to this emergency without being stressed. He could have put $50 per month in an account and called it "Car Maintenance Fund." At least that would have given him some money to use for the repairs. In a way, Darryl's car is an asset because it allows him to get to the job that provides him a steady income. Without it he risks losing his major income source and the foundation upon which his four pillars can be built. As you saw, two simple shifts in the way he operates—making better choices about his time, which is a resource, and creating a car maintenance reserve fund—can help him maintain the income that is vital on his path to financial liberty.

Here is another example of how income preservation is pivotal in the 4PFL process. Take Sherice, who works as customer service rep for a large cable company. Sherice is a twenty-four-year-old woman with a bachelor's degree in marketing. When she took the job with this cable company, her desire was to start in customer service but work her way into the marketing department, which in her interview she was told she could do. Sherice has been working at the company for two years and has grown extremely tired of dealing with the complaints from the customers. Although she is a customer service supervisor and she doesn't spend as much time on the phones as the twelve agents she supervises, this position is really not fulfilling for her.

One day while she is yelled at by her manager for not being able to satisfy an angry customer, Sherice gets fed up and, in anger, quits her job. She leaves the office with no notice and doesn't even explain to her managers why. Sherice has not examined how this hasty decision will affect her future, but the consequences for her actions are severe. First, she will deal with the loss of pay for the period it takes her to get a new job. Even if she got another job the day she left, there is a great chance she will not receive another paycheck for a minimum of three weeks. Sherice did not put away much money for savings, so she will likely finance this gap in pay by using credit cards. Second, she is going to have difficulty listing this job as a reference because of the way she left. Without solid references, her job search may not yield the results she is hoping for. She may have to settle for less money or take another job that is not fulfilling. Third, she has lost access to all the benefits that cable company provided, including medical and the company-sponsored 401K savings plan.

Sherice has not protected her income investment and, as a result, does not have a solid foundation on which to set her pillars. This lack of income means she is going to find it difficult to budget effectively. Her utilization of credit to finance this gap in income means she is sacrificing a solid personal credit score. She will not have much money to finance the basic expenses of starting a business if that is what she chooses to do, so there isn't a great possibility of establishing business credit. Again, she doesn't have much money, so acquiring assets is going to be next to impossible.

In those two scenarios we see how income is vitally important. There is an old saying, "Do what you have to do until you can do what you want to do." If we examine income creation and preservation and look at how it affects the four pillars, you probably recognize that this is the most logical starting point. In the first scenario, Darryl could have planned his time and budget a little better so that he wasn't in jeopardy of losing his job and had money in the budget to take care of the car. He also may have taken better care of the car, realizing that it was his way of getting access to his income. In the second example, Sherice could have considered where her income was before she stormed out of the job. Had she spoken to one of her supervisors about her frustrations and devised a plan for either moving ahead or moving on, she might have been able to stay employed at her current company, perhaps increasing her salary and protecting her retirement income.

The bottom line is that all finance is built on income. If we are talking about personal finance, then it is referred to as income. If we are talking about business finance, then it is called revenue. Either way, without income it is improbable that you are going to be able to establish an effective four-pillar way of building wealth. The tragedy in most minority cultures is that we don't have these conversations often, and if we do, we don't have them until late in life. These conversations should start with children; they can really begin as early as age five. Teach your kids that earning income and budgeting it wisely can lead to great rewards later in life. Teach them as early as possible how to earn income, how to budget it, and the importance of spending less and saving more *now* so that they can live in financial liberty later.

To begin to build wealth, it is necessary to understand the relationship between income and expenses as well. There is a simple equation that may help you to maintain a healthy income-to-expense ratio: Your TOTAL expenses should be no more than 55 percent of your TOTAL income. The reason the word "TOTAL" is capitalized here is because in order for this to really work, you have to include *all* your expenses in your equation, not just the major ones. Here is an example to explain this in detail. Terrence's monthly expenses follow:

Mortgage—$1,300
Utilities—$400
Cell phone—$100
Car note—$275
Car insurance—$125
Gasoline—$200
Groceries—$300
Entertainment—$300
Total—$3,000

Terrence's monthly income would have to be approximately $5,400 to maintain that ratio. If his income dipped below that number, Terrence could either do extra work to get his income back to those levels or reduce his expenses. He should probably do a combination of both to keep him comfortable.

Armed with this knowledge Terrence can make some important decisions. If he has been in his current position for three to four years and performed well, he might ask for a promotion and a raise. If he thinks his job may be in jeopardy, or if he has been in his position for a brief period, he may sit down with his managers to devise a personal development plan not only to ensure that he keeps his job but what steps he can take that might lead to a raise or promotion. At the very least, improving his performance will allow him to keep the job he has until he has something else lined up. He may decide to get another job that pays more or that he could have in addition to what he is doing. He may choose to refinance his home loan or car note for a lower rate. He may choose not to take on any additional unnecessary expenses, or he may reduce the cost of his expenses by choosing less-expensive options. Whatever he chooses, if he uses the 55 percent guideline, it will help him to set a great foundation for his four pillars.

Action

What are your financial goals?

This year? _____

Three years? _____

Five years? _____

Ten years? _____

Write down the names of all the people you know that have a net worth of $100K or more.

_____

_____

_____

_____

_____

If you had $1M to spend, write down all the things you would do with it.

_____

_____

_____

_____

_____

Write down all the books you have read in the last year that discuss wealth-building principles and what you learned from each.

_____

_____

_____

_____

_____

PART 2

PERSONAL FINANCE

Pillar 1

Budgeting Strategy

Now that we have a solid base of income upon which we can set our pillars, we can discuss each pillar in depth. The first pillar of financial liberty is budgeting. Many people cringe when they hear the word "budgeting" because they think they have to give up a great deal to gain little in return. The common thought is they must give up everything they like for a lengthy period. While it is true some sacrifices will have to be made, and you may have to forgo some of the things you enjoy for some period, you may already be budgeting but not seeing the benefits, which makes budgeting seem difficult.

Our view on budgeting is similar to those nutritionists who tell you that crash diets aren't extremely effective. Many people decide when they are going on a diet that they must give up all their favorite foods at once—bread, cookies, potatoes, macaroni, and cheese, and so on. What people don't quite understand is that quitting everything cold turkey leaves you craving for all of it. You may do well for a week or two, but then you are right back to eating those things. What's worse, people often overcompensate by overeating and do more damage than good to their bodies.

Finances are the same way. Many people start their budgets by cutting out every possible expense they can. At the same time, they attempt to save what seems to be huge chunks of money and to invest large amounts as well. It all works for a few months or so, but when the person realizes that his or her quality of life has gone down, the plan is abandoned. What is even more likely is that the plan goes well until the person has a major financial event, like refrigerator breaking, car problems, and unplanned social events. Once the person has to dip into the money he or she has been saving, it is hard to get back on track. It just becomes easier to forget about the plan altogether.

Before you consider making changes to your spending habits, it is helpful to understand the two types of budgeting: deficit budgeting and revenue budgeting. Following are descriptions of these terms:

Deficit Budgeting: Creating a budget that increases income by decreasing expenses.

Here is an example of deficit budgeting. Crystal is going to use the deficit budgeting method. One of the first things she does is make a list of *every* expense she has. She uses a spreadsheet, which is most effective for her, but if you are not familiar with spreadsheets, a plain piece of paper or accounting paper will do. Wherever you do it, just make sure you are writing things down. Notice that the word "every" is italicized above. That is because people often leave out minor expenses because they don't think they matter. But even a cup of coffee that you drink every day could shift your budget dramatically. Just consider if Crystal buys one cup of coffee five days per week that costs her $1.79 per cup, she is spending $8.95/week, $35/month, and $1,861/year. If Crystal makes $35K/year in salary, she is spending $1,861 of that on coffee. If her net pay after taxes, which is where her coffee budget comes from, is $27K/year, then she is spending $1,861 of that on coffee. Consider this: Most jobs, if they give you a raise every year, only give you a maximum of about a 5 percent increase in salary, which is $1,750 for Crystal. She is literally spending her raise on coffee. Crystal doesn't have to stop drinking coffee; she just needs to make sure she is accounting for it in her expenses.

Here is a list of common expenses, including some that many people don't account for regularly.

Expense	Monthly Cost
Mortgage/Rent (including insurance)	$1,369
Car note (including insurance)	$548
Student loans	$439
Utilities	$270
Cable	$130
Credit cards	$80
Groceries	$300
Clothing (including purchased clothing and dry cleaning)	$250
Hair	$110
Restaurants (including fast food)	$200
Travel (including tolls and gas)	$200
Miscellaneous	$150
Total	$4,046

Once every expense has been listed, Crystal can begin tracking her spending. It might be helpful for her to get an app that allows her to monitor her income and expenses. A simple check register app will do, but she can use more elaborate ones as well. Crystal will take one month and begin recording every expense she has for that month. As mentioned previously, it is extremely important that she records all her expenses, even the minor ones. For example, it may not seem important to note when she has purchased a pack of gum or an ice cream cone. But at the end of the month, she is going to compare her estimated expenses to her actual expenses. In other words, she will take the list she created and compare it to the list of expenses she actually had during the month and note the differences. If Crystal did this for her first month, she may be shocked that even though her estimated expenses were roughly $4,046, she actually spent $4,291, a difference of $245. She hadn't made more income but found herself spending outside her budget. To be clear, part of that was because she estimated her electric bill to be one amount, but it came in at approximately $40 more for that month. She had also done this with some other bills. This is not uncommon but doing this exercise can help her adjust. A good piece of advice is to increase the estimates of some bills and leave the ones that never changed as budgeted before. For example, her car note always remains the same, so she did not need to adjust the budget for that. If she wants to be certain of her monthly expenses, she may want to track for sixty or ninety days just to see where some major differences may lie.

Most people who live in places where weather changes seasonally see their utility bills differ from season to season. For example, people living in the Northeast United States may find that their electric bill is higher in the winter than in the summer or vice versa, depending on air-conditioning usage. Tracking over a longer period lets you see how to average those things out.

Once Crystal has collected and studied the data, meaning she knows what her monthly expenses are, she can take action. Once again, she can start this part of the plan with deficit budgeting. She can take a look at all her expenses and start to make changes to lower them. Some of the expenses listed below are easier to redo:

- *Cable bill*: See if she can use a combination of streaming services that will allow her to lower her bill.
- *Cell phone*: See if she can switch to a lower monthly plan.

- *Restaurants*: Give herself a weekly allowance that is less than what she currently spends on restaurants.
- *Car insurance*: See if she can get a better rate.
- *Car payment*: See if she can refinance for a lower payment.

Let's say all of Crystal's expenses totaled $4,046/month before she made adjustments. Then she decreased them to $3,856/month, a savings of $190. She shouldn't take that savings of $190 and spend it. Instead, she could spend 25 percent ($47.50) on herself, a reward for making the adjustments, and the other 75 percent ($142.50) could be put toward paying off some debt. For example, take $50/month and use it to treat herself to an extra dinner per month, and take the other $140 and pay off her credit card debt, car payment, student loan, and so on.

Credit cards are also part of her expenses. I am going to cover personal credit in the next pillar, but for now we'll discuss it as it relates to budgeting. Once Crystal has reduced her expenses, she can focus on her credit card debt. When addressing credit card bills, "debt stacking" has been an extremely effective method for many. Debt stacking is using the extra money gained by paying off one debt to pay off the next until all debt is paid. For example, following is a breakdown of the four credit cards Crystal has:

Card Name	Initial Balance	Owed Balance	Available Balance	Monthly Payment
Capital One	$500	$175	$325	$25
Credit One	$1,000	$780	$220	$50
Macy's	$2,500	$2,465	$35	$100
Visa	$5,000	$1,700	$3,300	$100

In this example, Crystal would begin her budget by paying off the owed balance on Capital One. Once she does that, she will have another $175 (owed balance) in her available budget, and her monthly expenses will have decreased by $25 (monthly payment). Since she is already used to paying that $25/month, she would not take it and blow it. Instead, she would apply it to the monthly payment of Credit One, which changes that amount to $75/month, effectively paying off the balance of Credit One sooner.

Assuming no interest accrues on the balance of Credit One, and she only paid the monthly payment of $50, it would take her 15.5 months to pay off the owed balance of $780. However, if she made the monthly payment of $75, it would take her 10.5 months. She could even apply any extra money she got from working overtime or taxes or selling unwanted tech items in her home to paying off the balances and decrease her debt even faster. She would continue applying this principle to each of the four cards until they were all paid off. It is important to note that once she pays the card off, she *should not* run up the balance again, or she will be in this perpetual loop and never get out of debt. But she doesn't want to cancel the cards altogether. The reason for that will be explained in the credit component of these four pillars.

Revenue budgeting: Creating a budget that increases income by increasing revenues.

Once Crystal has lowered all her expenses as much as possible and applied the debt-stacking principle, it is time to explore revenue budgeting. In revenue budgeting, we do everything in our power to increase the money we bring in, or at least save more of the money we are bringing in. Ask yourself this question: How can I save more of the money I am already bringing in? Here are a few methods that have worked extremely well for many people.

The first method is the coin bottle. This method is extremely specific, and it is suggested that you take that into account. Purchase a five-gallon water bottle from a store that sells water, like Walmart or Costco. Here are the specs on that bottle and why they are important:

- Five gallon—so it holds many coins
- Glass—so it is heavy, and you are not tempted to pick it up and dump it out often
- Clear—so you can see your money as it accumulates
- Thin necked—so you can't reach your hand inside and take out the coins

Fig. 7 Coin Bottle

Not only can you use that bottle to collect your coins, but you can also be extremely deliberate in how you collect those coins. When paying cash for items, many people will pay the exact amount if they have it. For instance, if you purchase a pack of gum for $1.39 (I can't believe gum, costs $1.39 a pack ... ridiculous), and you have a dollar bill and forty cents in your pocket. You will give the cashier that money and receive one penny back in change. Instead, consider using two paper dollars to pay for that gum so you can have the sixty-one cents in change in addition to the forty cents already in your pocket. That means when you get home, you would be dumping at least $1.01 in change into the jar. In addition, not only could you get your change from this transaction, but if you had another dollar bill in your pocket at the time, you could ask for change for that dollar. Now you have $2.01 to put into the bottle. As you can see, that is now a two-dollar difference in the amount that you put into the bottle, and it didn't really affect your day tremendously. Once you start filling up this bottle with change, and you see the level start to rise, it will motivate you to keep going.

The effectiveness of this method is not just in the collection but in the spending. As I said before, you become motivated to collect more and more change as you see the levels rise. It may work well if you start this collection on January 1, and then keep collecting throughout the year. On December 20—specifically December 20—exchange those coins for dollars at one of the coin-exchange outlets. You can then take that money and use it to purchase something nice for someone in your family for the holidays. Or buy yourself something that you wanted throughout the year but never purchased, like a watch or a pair of sneakers, things that you like to have. Often those coins amount to well over $350 during the year. This means that you can buy things that you normally wouldn't have had in the budget, which is more motivation to start all over again next year.

Another technique is the cashbox. Again, the effectiveness of this technique is in how you spend the money. Get yourself a small cashbox from any office supply store. The dimensions are not as important as the coin bottle, but you may want to get something that is relatively easy to lift and move around. You can choose one with a lock on it, but locking it is not absolutely necessary unless you are concerned that people in your house are not as trustworthy as you would like them to be. This technique is called the "paper dollar excess" technique because of how you use it to accumulate money. Anytime you have paper dollars above an amount divisible by five, put them into this lockbox. For example, if you have seventeen dollars in your pocket, take two singles and put them into the cashbox. Likewise, if you have twenty-four dollars, put four singles into the cashbox. The difficult task here is asking you not to spend those singles because they are a significant part of your everyday spending. However, all savings techniques require that you change habits, which really means changing how you think. If you can do that, this can work.

It is important to note that you shouldn't make a habit of frequently counting the singles in the cashbox. That money will start to accumulate very quickly and counting it will only tempt you to use it, making the technique useless.

Fig. 8 Cashbox

Just like you did with the coin bottle, you are going to exchange those singles for large bills on December 20. However, you may want to use that money to travel with instead of buying items. A study of the wealthiest people on earth revealed that over 80 percent of them take at least three vacations per year (Scobel, n.d). That is because it allows your mind, body, and soul to get the much-needed rest and relaxation it needs. A common misunderstanding is that people are not in a financial position to take even one vacation, let alone three. But this technique allows you some extra income to put toward a vacation or something else. On average, even with a modest income, you should be able to save about $450 during a year using this tactic. No, that is not going to pay for a full vacation on a tropical island, but it can allow you to pay for a round-trip flight to the island. If you use this money in addition to other money-saving techniques, you can travel like you desire. Following are some quick travel tips that have been used over the years:

- Choose off days to fly to and from your destination. For example, fly out on a Tuesday and come back on a Thursday.
- Fly to destinations during the off-season. For example, go to Chicago during the winter months.
- Fly using less-expensive airlines (Frontier) and from airports that are not major hubs (Trenton-Mercer).
- Book your trip as far in advance as possible.
- Use Groupon to book your excursions and events while you are on vacation.
- Use Airbnb to save on hotel stays while you are on vacation.
- Book entertainment on off days and in advance.

The key to all these things is to create a normal budget for them. Then take the extra money you saved by using these tips and put it in a savings account. For example, if Malcolm were going on a three-day vacation trip to Chicago, his normal budget may look like this:

Flight—$400
Hotel—$300
Car rental—$150

Spending—$150
Total—$1,000

However, by using the techniques above, that trip may cost the following:

Flight—$200
Airbnb—$150
Car rental—$100
Spending—$150
Total—$600

By doing it this way, Malcolm saved four hundred dollars. Instead of spending that extra four hundred, he would put it in a savings account. Maybe he wouldn't put all of it in savings either. It's possible he could take half of that money and put it in savings and use the other half to enhance the trip—buy more clothes for the trip, do an extra excursion on the trip, eat at a better-quality restaurant, and so on. The point is, he would still have some savings and could enjoy himself even more.

Here are a few more unorthodox money-saving techniques:

- Couponing
- Buying from thrift stores
- Getting building materials from places like the Restore

These are all methods to reduce what is called "buyer's remorse." This happens when you buy something that is outside your budget and then regret it. Many people experience this and don't actually enjoy what they bought because they have anxiety about spending outside the budget. These methods help to reduce anxiety because it feels as if you are using free money. Although obviously there is no such thing as free money, you have made a small but effective adjustment to how you utilize money during the year.

Now that we have talked about how to utilize some unorthodox techniques for saving, we are going to discuss the more traditional methods of saving money, but they focus on mindset change. One of the first things you can do to save more money is change the way you prioritize savings and spending. Most people you use their paychecks in this order: (1) bills, (2) everyday living, (3) spending, and (4) savings. The disadvantage of this way of life is that they typically don't have anything left for savings because it becomes less important. Let's say Malcolm's paycheck was $2,000. Bills may equal a thousand dollars, and then he must account for everyday living: groceries, travel and transportation, child-care expenses, and so on. That may equal five hundred dollars. He then spends another five hundred on entertainment, clothing, or items that are unaccounted for, such as tires for the car. When all is said and done, the two thousand dollars is spent long before he gets to savings.

But if he switches priorities, then his mindset shifts, and he starts living toward financial liberty. Most people are motivated by bills. We do whatever it takes to get them paid because it means keeping the lights on, the water running, the cell phone operating, and the rent paid. That said, the suggestion is that you switch the order. Take that $2,000 and put the first $250 into savings; in other words, pay yourself first. Put the next five hundred into a spending account that you will use for entertainment, clothing, or items that are unaccounted for, like tires for the car. Then take the next five hundred and pay everyday living expenses. You are left with $750, but your bills amount to $1,000. Again, we typically do whatever we can to cover our bills, so this should motivate you to do whatever it takes to make up the $250 difference. Here are some of the things you can do to make up that difference:

- Lower your expenses by $250. Look at your spending and see where you can make the reductions.
- Sell items that you no longer use but may have value to someone else (for example, old cell phones, and bicycles).
- Get a part-time job driving for Uber/Lyft, delivering food for Door Dash/GrubHub or traditional, like for Walmart.

Switching priorities also keeps people motivated to go forward. How many times have you walked into work and been unhappy? Some of that unhappiness is a result of putting in all the hours but not being able to enjoy the money you make. When you are working but not seeing your savings grow or not being able to travel or enjoy entertainment, it is a demotivator. Once you have lowered your monthly expenses as much as you can, started using the simple money-saving techniques, and found creative ways to increase your revenue, it is time to focus on your credit.

Budgeting is an exercise, just like push-ups are exercises. It is not necessary that you attempt to do everything all at once. Take baby steps through the process until you've built up enough financial muscle that you can go on to the bigger steps. You don't have to choose deficit budgeting or revenue budgeting; you can choose both. However, it may be most comfortable to address one at a time so you can better focus.

Action

Fill out the following table as accurately as you can. If you need more space, you can write the information on a separate piece of paper.

Income Statement			
Income			
Description	Cash Flow ($)		
	$_____		
	$_____		
	$_____		
Real Estate			
	$_____		
	$_____		
	$_____		
Businesses			

	$_____		
	$_____		
	$_____	**Total Income**	$_____
Expenses			
	$_____		
	$_____		
	$_____		
	$_____		
	$_____		
	$_____		
	$_____		
	$_____		
	$_____		
	$_____		
	$_____		
	$_____	**Total Expenses**	$_____
	$_____		
	$_____		
	$_____	**Paycheck (Total Income – Total Expenses)**	
			$_____

In the table below, write down all expenses that you can reduce.

	Current Amount	Reduced Amount	Savings
	$_____	$_____	$_____
	$_____	$_____	$_____
	$_____	$_____	$_____
	$_____	$_____	$_____
	$_____	$_____	$_____
	$_____	$_____	$_____
	$_____	$_____	$_____
	$_____	$_____	$_____
Total	$_____	$_____	$_____

Note: Take 25 percent of savings and spend it on whatever you like as a reward for reducing expenses. You will invest the other 75 percent when you get to the "Asset Acquisition" section of this book.

In the table below, write down your credit card information.

Card Name	Initial Balance	Owed Balance	Available Balance	Monthly Payment
	$_____	$_____	$_____	$_____
	$_____	$_____	$_____	$_____
	$_____	$_____	$_____	$_____
	$_____	$_____	$_____	$_____
	$_____	$_____	$_____	$_____
	$_____	$_____	$_____	$_____
	$_____	$_____	$_____	$_____
	$_____	$_____	$_____	$_____
	$_____	$_____	$_____	$_____
	$_____	$_____	$_____	$_____
	$_____	$_____	$_____	$_____

Get coin bottle.

Fig. 7 Coin Bottle

Remember, the specs of this bottle are important, so consider the following when choosing your bottle:

- Should be clear so you can see the accumulation.
- Should be a glass bottle so it's heavy.
- Should have a narrow neck so you can't fit your hand in it.
- Should be at least five gallons so you can collect lots of coins.
- Instead of using exact change to make purchases, get the change. For example, if your purchase is $2.16 give them $3 instead of $2.16. You'll accumulate even more and faster if you ask for an additional dollar's worth of quarters with every purchase.

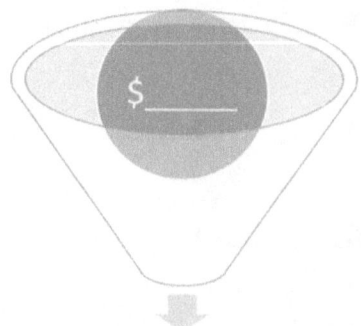

Write how much change you have on
December 20th on the line above

Try not to take any of the change out of the bottle until December 20.

Get cash box.

Fig. 8 Cashbox

This is where you will store your dollar bills. Remember the specs are important as well.

- Should be lightweight so you can lift it to put the money inside.
- Should have a lock on it so you can prevent theft.
- Should have rubber bands so you can stack the bills in groups of $25.

Remember, try not to use any of the money until December 20. Write the amount of money you have on December 20 on the line below.

 $_____

Pillar 2

Personal Credit

Fig. 9 Personal Credit

Unless you have been living in a cave for the past two hundred years, you are probably aware that a significant portion of your financial picture is connected to your credit profile. There is no disputing that. In the United States there is a great deal of emphasis placed on a consumer's creditworthiness. For example, your credit score and profile are used to determine whether you can get a mortgage and what the interest rate will be and your ability to buy a car and what your insurance rates are. They can even affect the outcome of your job applications. Those individuals with the best credit have access to many more financial resources than others. Jay-Z often quotes Warren Buffet when he says, "I rarely have enough cash to buy a full tank of gas, but I have enough credit to buy the gas station."

Many people think credit is a bad thing, but it is probably because we are calling it credit. It is much closer to being debt than credit. The issue is in the definitions and context of credit and debt. In its purest form, credit means that you have overpaid for something, and someone owes you money back. You can leverage that money owed to you later in life. Debt is just the opposite; this means that you owe someone more than he or she owes you, and the person or business can leverage that debt at a later time.

When we discuss credit and creditworthiness, we are really saying how much debt people are willing to extend you and how likely you are to pay it back. Debt comes in the forms of credit cards, personal loans, auto loans, student loans, and so on. People often get into trouble when they take on this debt but then are unable to repay or can't pay on time. The result is poor credit ratings and a limited ability to obtain more credit. What's worse is it takes considerably longer to build good credit than it does to destroy it.

Understanding Your Credit Score

Let's talk about your credit score and how it is determined. There are many bureaus that calculate your credit score, but there are three major ones: Equifax, Experian, and TransUnion. I bet you didn't know that these agencies are not governmental entities and are not regulated by a governmental body. Instead, they are private, for-profit entities. In other words, they make money by selling credit information to other companies. What this means to you is that they sell your personal information, including address and Social Security number, to companies that can use this information any way they choose. In addition, they don't have to protect your privacy or to report accurately, so it is up to you to see that they do so.

These three agencies, along with the Fair Isaac Corporation (FICO), have developed a credit rating mechanism called a FICO score. That FICO score ranges from 350, the lowest, to 850, the highest, and is made up of five factors:

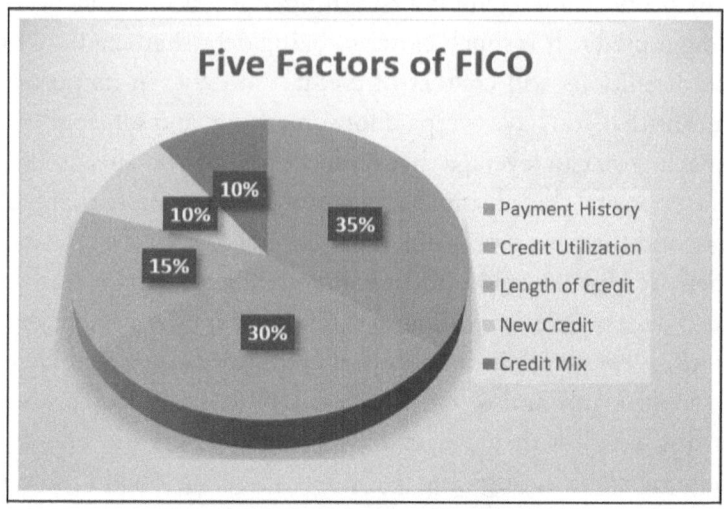

Payment History—35 percent
Credit Utilization—30 percent
Length of Credit History—15 percent
New Credit—10 percent
Credit Mix—10 percent

Fig. 10 Five Factors of a FICO Score

As you can see, the five factors are weighted, which means each factor affects your credit score differently than the rest. One of the most frustrating aspects of credit for people is that they work really hard to maintain positive status on one or two of the factors, but their scores don't increase significantly. That is because those factors may not be weighted as heavily as the rest.

Now let's explain each of the five factors and talk about things you need pay attention to.

Payment history means the record of all your credit payments made. Not everything you make payments on shows up on your credit report. Things like credit cards, car loans, student loans, and mortgages will show up, but things like cell phones, electric bills, and rent will not. If you make a late payment on the things that do show up, it negatively impacts your score. If you don't pay on an account at all and it goes into collection, that will negatively impact your score. In fact, that will show up twice because you will have the delinquent payment show up, and the collection account will show up.

It is extremely important that you pay all your bills on time. The more payments you make on time, the better your credit standing will be. You must understand that it takes much longer to repair a negative history than it does to destroy a positive history. For example, if you make one late payment on your student loans, your credit score could drop by thirty points in thirty days. However, it may take you six months to a year of paying that same student loan on time to increase your score by that same thirty points. The message here is that paying your credit bills on time is the most critical component in keeping your credit in good standing.

Credit utilization means the amount of credit you have used compared to the credit limit. For example, if you have a credit card that has credit limit of $1,000 and you have used $800, then your credit utilization is 80 percent. Conversely, if you only use $300 on that same card, your credit utilization is 30 percent. Most credit counselors agree that a credit utilization of 30 percent or less is a great number to strive for. Does this mean you can only use $300 of the $1,000 on that credit card? The tough answer is yes. However, you can also use the reporting date to your advantage. The reporting date is the date the credit card company reports your balances to the credit bureaus. You can use all $1,000 of that available limit in a payment cycle as long as you can pay back at least $700 of that balance before the reporting date. The key is knowing what that reporting date is and making sure you have the money available beforehand. This is why many people with great credit choose American Express charge cards. Those cards require you pay the balance in full before the reporting date. In order to take full advantage of this technique, we strongly encourage you to contact your credit card companies and ask them what their reporting dates are.

Length of credit history means the amount of time you maintain your credit. Having items on your credit report for a minimum of seven years is a great way to increase your credit standing as long as those things are being reported as positive. For example, if you have a credit card for fifteen years and have always paid the balance on time, this will help tremendously. That is typically why people with mortgages have higher credit scores. Mortgages have longer payment cycles and are usually priority for people, which is why they get are generally paid before all else.

What negatively affects your credit age the most is paying off credit cards and then closing the accounts. For example, a person may have gotten a Visa card seven years ago with a $1,000 credit limit. The person used all $1,000 of that limit, and for most of those seven years paid the minimum monthly payments. At some point the individual received a lump sum of money and decided to pay that credit card balance in full. This is a great idea, but if the person closes the account after paying off that balance, that card is no longer being reported. In short, the seven-year history with that account is erased, which actually hurts the individual.

New credit means any recent items that have been added to your credit report. They are also called "hard inquiries." If you have applied for a credit card, car loan, mortgage, and so on in the last twelve months, that would be considered new credit. This affects your credit in two ways. The first is that you haven't built a positive history on that credit yet, so it doesn't help to increase your score. It may not decrease your score either, but you want to do everything in your power to increase your credit rating as much as possible. Where it has a huge impact is on the credit inquiry component of credit. When a potential creditor runs your credit, a "hard pull" or a "soft pull" can be used. A hard pull means they are using all the information in your credit profile to determine creditworthiness, and this has a negative impact on your score. It can often drop your score by ten points or more. A soft pull means the potential creditor is only using partial information, and it doesn't impact your score at all. In addition, if you have too many inquiries in a given period, that can have a negative impact on your credit rating. Two things to consider when applying for credit: (1) always ask the creditor if it will be a hard pull or a soft pull, and (2) if you must apply for new credit and are soliciting different lenders, do all the inquiries in one thirty-day period instead of spreading it out over multiple thirty-day periods. Credit bureaus look at all the inquiries in one thirty-day period as one inquiry. It is important to note that most inquiries will fall off your credit reports exactly two years to the date of when it was pulled. Once the inquiry comes off, your credit score typically goes up by three to five points. Keep that in mind and use it to your advantage.

Credit mix means the types of credit that shows up on your credit report. There are three basic types: installment, revolving, and open. Installment is credit that has a fixed monthly payment that does not change. The total amount borrowed is paid back over a fixed period of the same amount monthly. An example of installment credit is your mortgage. Revolving credit has a different payment amount every month based on the amount you use. This credit allows you to pay a portion of the minimum balance due and push the other portion into the next month, changing the amount due. An example of revolving credit is a credit card. Open is credit whose full balance is due every month. These accounts charge interest or fees if the balance is not paid in full by the due date. These types of accounts can often lead to loss of privileges if not paid in full. An example of open credit is an American Express charge card. People with credit scores above 780 typically have at least one of each of these types of credit. They usually come in the form of a mortgage (installment), three major credit cards (revolving), and an American Express card (open).

Now that we have explained the credit factors that are used to calculate a credit score, you should be able to use them to your advantage. When repairing credit, some people have chosen to address the items on their report that negatively impact their payment history first, since this is the most heavily weighted factor. Keep in mind that these items have a history, so it is a time-bound factor. In other words, it may take you months—even years—to reverse the effects of this negative history. However, if any of those items are being reported inaccurately, our suggestion is that you dispute them early in your credit repair process.

Let's conclude this section by discussing credit repair. While I won't go in depth, I will tell you that credit repair is *not* a hopeless endeavor. Countless people have literally given up on repairing their credit. They have just decided they are never going to have access to some of the things that come to those with great credit. Hopefully, this reading can encourage you. Good credit repair agencies and counselors have helped people with credit scores that were in the low 400s get unsecured credit cards, car loans, and even mortgages. They have also helped people overcome major negative items like bankruptcy, repossession, and student loan default.

What we really want to impress upon you is that credit repair is unique to every individual. Many credit repair companies will tell you that they can give you typical results. Be careful when working with those companies because two people can have the same credit score, but it can take one of those people one month to raise that credit score by fifty points and the other person a year to do the same. The results you get depend on a variety of things including, of course, the five factors we just discussed. Everyone can repair their own credit scores and do it legally. However, we strongly suggest you get assistance from someone who has done it successfully or work with a company that specializes in it. Although you probably could do your own taxes, the professionals generally have access to knowledge and expertise that you can benefit from.

Repairing Your Credit

Now how selfish would I be if I gave you information about personal credit without giving you a plan for repairing it if necessary? The first step is to obtain credit reports. There are many providers of credit reports, and there aren't any endorsements given here. But the most effective ones will give you access to all three credit bureaus. Experience suggests that a monthly fee of $9.95 to $19.95 is what you can expect from some of the most popular ones. You can get access to free credit reports, but some of those services may have limitations. I suggest that you use a service that gives you credit monitoring, so you can review your scores and reports periodically and see what changes occur. In addition, it should give scores, account numbers, and contact information for your creditors.

Once you have pulled your credit reports the next step is to review them thoroughly for errors and inaccuracies. Statistics show that over 79 percent of credit reports contain errors. These are the easiest to fix and can help boost your score relatively quickly. If names, dates, amounts, and account numbers aren't correct, you can use those errors to your advantage. Keep in mind that the Fair Credit Reporting Act (FCRA) allows you, as the consumer, to dispute any errors on your credit report. Writing letters to dispute these errors may seem like a daunting task, but you can always find examples on the internet. This can't be emphasized enough: You can fix your own credit, but a credit counseling professional is a great resource because he or she should know the laws of credit repair and how to prepare letters that will get results.

Next, you can write letters to the credit bureaus to remove all the derogatory information that is dated more than seven years in the past. The FCRA also states that any derogatory claims on your credit report that are dated more than seven years in the past can be removed at the consumer's request. There is a common misconception that this happens automatically. That could not be further from the truth. Let's say Corey has a medical bill of $4,535 that has remained unpaid for seven years. Neither the medical company that owns the debt nor the credit bureaus have an obligation to remove that debt from Corey's credit report. It is Corey's obligation to write a letter to have that item removed.

Once you have addressed the inaccuracies and the outdated items, the next step is to use the FCRA to help you with companies that will not be able to respond to inquiries within a thirty-day period. The law says that a company has thirty days to respond to inquiries made by a consumer. If the company is unable to respond within that thirty-day window, the derogatory information should be removed from the credit reports. There are many companies that don't have mechanisms in place to be able to respond to those inquiries in time, and you can use that to your advantage. It is imperative, though, that you send letters by certified mail so that you have a receipt of the date you mailed it and an assurance that the company received it. Track the dates on your certified mail receipts, and if the company doesn't respond in thirty days, send a second letter to the credit bureaus with proof that they didn't respond, and ask the credit bureaus to remove the derogatory information from your credit report.

Once you have completed these steps, what is left are accounts that actually belong to you and are reporting accurately. The last step is to settle your collection accounts. This might be difficult to believe, but collection agencies often settle accounts for much less than you owe. Before you learn how to get them to do this, you may be interested in why they do it. Collection agencies buy debt for pennies on the dollar. Here's how it works. Let's say Tameka has a Capital One card that she owed $1,000 on, and that balance went into collection. Capital One can write up to 75 percent of that balance off on their taxes (charge off), so they only have to pay taxes on $250 of the balance. That $250 gets sold to CCS Collections for $300, effectively netting Capital One a $50 profit. CCS Collections then calls Tameka and attempts to settle that debt for $600, earning CCS a $300 profit if she pays. Tameka can leverage this knowledge with CCS into settling the debt for much less than they propose. If you look at the math, CCS will earn 100 percent profit on their investment if Tameka pays. However, they are likely willing to settle for less because there is a risk to them that Tameka won't pay any of the debt. It is better for them to collect something than nothing at all.

This is where the leverage comes in. A letter should be written to CCS, asking it to settle for less than the amount they are proposing. This, of course, is determined by Tameka's budget. The letter should state that CCS is agreeing to settle for the amount indicated in the letter, and it should be accompanied with a check for the proposed amount. The letter should state, "If CCS cashes this check, then it is a binding agreement to settle the debt for the amount on the check." The letter should also state that "This constitutes payment in full, and the derogatory will be removed from all three credit bureau reports." Of course, that letter should be sent certified mail. If there is no response in thirty days, or if CCS doesn't agree to the terms, Tameka should keep writing letters and sending checks for different amounts until CCS agrees.

Personal credit is necessary, but it doesn't have to be a taboo topic. Many African Americans despise credit because they have been disproportionately subject to unfair credit practices. However, there are laws in place that can protect us if we know how to use them. In addition, there are strategies that can be put in place to ensure the credit scores you desire and can help you to maintain them. Here are just a few tips:

- Pay all your bills on time or before they are due.
- Know the interest rates, due dates, reporting dates, and fees associated with all credit cards.
- Never use more than 25 percent of the credit limits on cards.
- Never close any credit voluntarily, especially if you have had it for more than seven years. Just pay it off and don't use it.
- Ask any creditor if they can use a soft pull instead of a hard pull to grant you credit.
- If you are applying for new credit, do it all in one thirty-day period.
- Make sure you have at least one credit account in each of the three credit categories: installment, revolving, and open.
- Settle all collection accounts, and make sure the collection agency removes the negative entry from all three credit bureaus.

One other important principle that we must address is how you communicate with your creditors. There are certainly differing opinions on this topic, but the most effective credit repair companies in the country almost always communicate via postal mail. This method is effective because many creditors don't have a system of addressing postal mail in a timely manner, which can work to your advantage. Here are some pointers you can use when addressing your creditors:

- Send every correspondence with them via certified mail.
- If they do not respond within thirty days, send a follow-up letter with the proof of the first correspondence to the three credit bureaus (Equifax, Experian, and TransUnion), asking them to remove the derogatory from your credit report.
- *Do not* communicate via phone call.
- Attempt to settle collection accounts for 25 percent of the balance. If the creditors don't agree, keep negotiating, but never go higher that 50 percent of the balance. Note: If you have the total balance in your budget, you should pay it. But make sure you send a check via mail, and *do not* pay over the phone.
- Keep a file of all your correspondence.

While you may not like the fact that we live in a credit society, you are certainly subject to that fact, so mastering the techniques for using it are definitely advantageous.

Action

What is your current credit score?

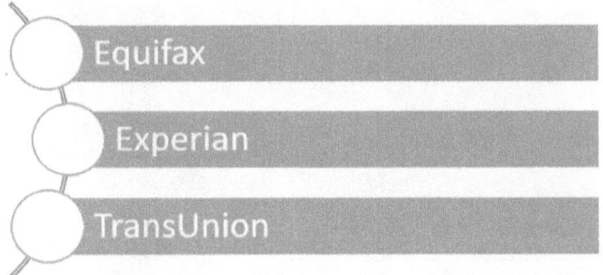

What would you like your credit scores to be?

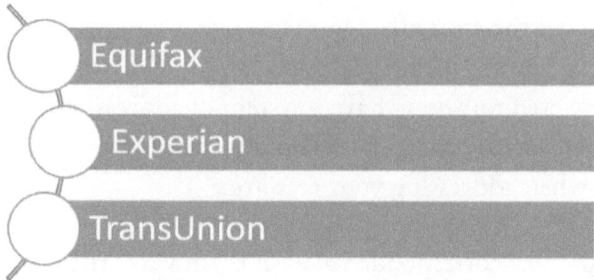

Which of the following are you looking to purchase in the next twelve months? (Check all that apply.)

☐ House
☐ Car
☐ Business
☐ Assets
☐ None of the above

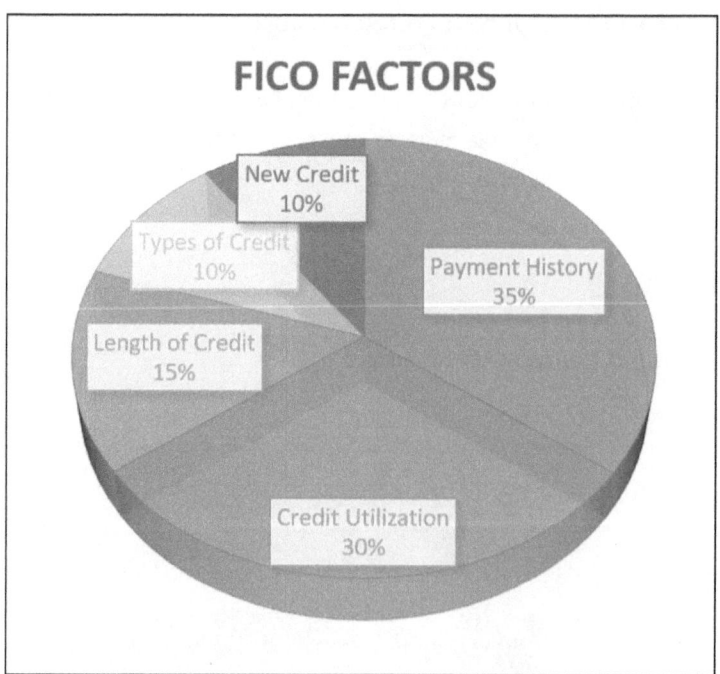

Payment history refers to how you pay your creditors. Paying them on or before the due dates will increase your credit score, while paying late or missing payments will decrease your credit score.

List any accounts for which you have either paid late or missed a payment.

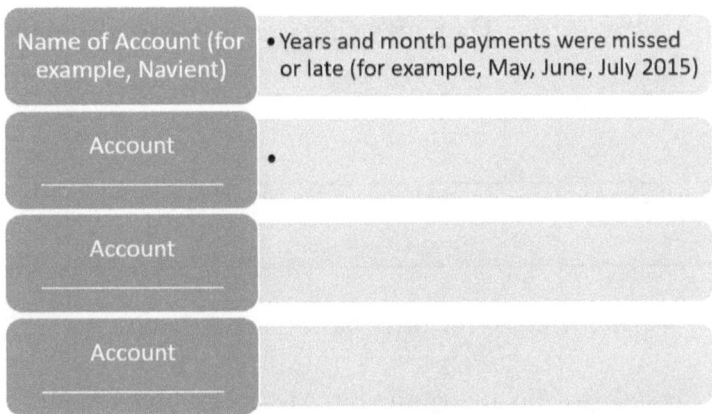

Name of Account (for example, Navient)	• Years and month payments were missed or late (for example, May, June, July 2015)
Account _____	•
Account _____	
Account _____	

Credit utilization refers to what you owe relative to the account's credit limit. For example, if you have a credit card with a credit limit of $1,000 and have used $450 of it, your utilization is 45 percent. The recommended credit utilization rate is 25 percent or below.

List all your credit cards, their credit limits, and the amounts owed.

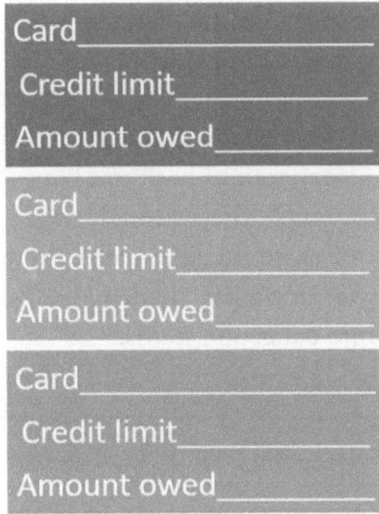

Card_____
Credit limit_____
Amount owed_____

Card_____
Credit limit_____
Amount owed_____

Card_____
Credit limit_____
Amount owed_____

Length of credit refers to the amount of time you have had your credit accounts. Having an open account for seven years or more looks most favorable on your credit report. It is good to pay account balances off but leave the account open.

List all accounts you have that have been opened seven years or more.

Name of Account	Date Opened	Account Balance

Types of credit refers to the three basic types of credit:

Revolving—You are required to pay a minimum amount of your balance each month. If you choose to do so, the remaining balance will be rolled over (revolved) into the next month. In some cases, the balance is subject to a higher interest rate. An example of this is a credit card.

Installment—You are required to pay a fixed sum each month based on factors such as total amount borrowed, the time of the loan, and the decided-upon interest rate. An example of this is a mortgage.

Open—You are required to pay a fixed balance in full each month. As opposed to both revolving accounts and installment accounts, these usually don't charge any interest. Most of these accounts don't show up on your credit unless you don't pay them for a time, and your account goes into collection status.

People with credit scores above 720 typically have at least one of each on their credit reports, and they keep them in good standing. An example of this is a cell phone.

List all the accounts you have for each of the credit types.

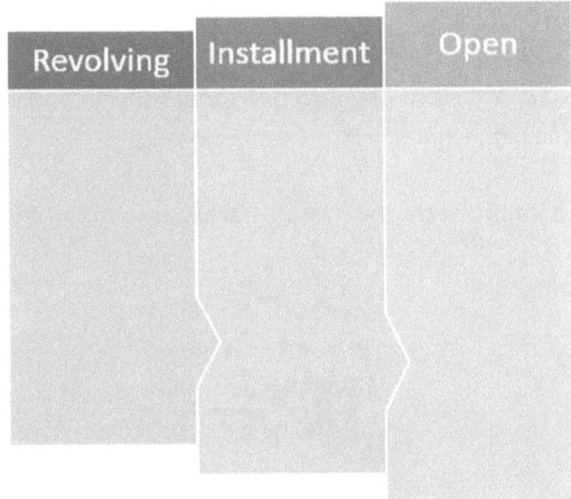

If you are missing any of these, please fill in the table below.

What type of credit (revolving, installment, or open)?	What do you plan to get (for example, mortgage, credit card, cell phone)?	When do you plan to get it (for example, June 15, 2022?	How much will it cost (for example, $102K)?

New credit refers to the inquiries that show up on your credit report. There are two types of credit pulls:

> *Hard pull*—When a creditor checks your credit with the three credit bureaus (Equifax, Experian, and TransUnion). Each pull represents a reduction in credit scores of three

to five points but will come off your credit two years after they are pulled.

Soft pull—When a creditor pulls credit from some secondary sources. They do not show up on your credit report but may not give an accurate account of your credit.

List all the inquiries that will expire in the next six months.

Account name_____
Date it will be removed_____

Account name_____
Date it will be removed_____

Account name_____
Date it will be removed_____

Go to the following links and create accounts:

IdentityIQ: https://www.identityiq.com/creditpreferred.aspx?offercode=431141EH

CreditKarma: https://www.creditkarma.com/dashboard

In the following table, track your credit scores for the next twelve months. On the first of each month, list your credit scores for each bureau.

	Equifax	Experian	TransUnion
January			
February			
March			
April			
May			
June			
July			
August			
September			
October			
November			
December			

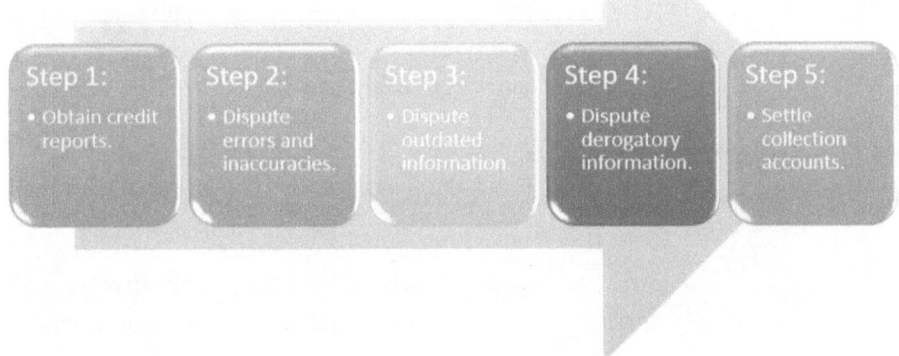

Step 1:
• Obtain credit reports.

Step 2:
• Dispute errors and inaccuracies.

Step 3:
• Dispute outdated information.

Step 4:
• Dispute derogatory information.

Step 5:
• Settle collection accounts.

Following is a sample credit analysis. Use this to help determine what steps you can do to boost your personal credit and how to do those steps.

1. Payment History
   a. Capital One—Late payment dates 2020: April–June
   b. Macy's—Late payment dates 2020: April–July

    c.   Navient—Late payment dates 2020: September–October
        i.   Write letters asking for removal of derogatory status.

Make sure you pay *all* your bills on time or early.

2.   Credit Utilization

Name of Creditor	Credit Limit	Balance Owed	Pay at Least	Never Use More Than …
Barclay's	$2,500	$2,439	$1,800	$625

Never use more than 25 percent of the available balance.
Pay the balance at least five days before the due date.

3.   Length of Credit
    a.   The average age of your credit is four years and two months.
    b.   Creditors like to see an average age of seven years or more, so you just have to wait.
    c.   Don't close any accounts.
        i.   You can pay off items, but don't close the accounts.
    d.   Do not open any new accounts.
        i.   This will reduce your score dramatically.

4.   New Credit (Hard Inquiries)
    a.   Comcast: 09/20/20
    b.   COAF: 10/29/20
        i.   Write letters asking for early removal of these inquiries.
        ii.   Please don't apply for any new credit until you have finished fixing your credit

5.   Credit Mix
    a.   You have at least one line of credit in each of the following categories:
        i.   Installment (student loans)
        ii.   Revolving (credit card: Capital One)

iii. Open (none). Work to get credit in this category (American Express Card). Your scores should be 700 or higher before you apply

Make sure you know all the details of what you are applying for, including interest rate, fees, payment due date, reporting date).

Don't miss a payment or make a late payment on that credit.

6. Settlements

Collection Agency	Original Creditor	Amount Owed	Amount Settled
Convergent	Sprint	$1,195	$600

   a. Write letters to get these removed.
   b. If they don't get removed, try to negotiate with the collection agencies for the "amount settled."

7. Charge Offs

Creditor	Amount Owed	Date Closed
WFDS	$7,915	05/14/17

Just monitor this account to make sure it doesn't go to collection.

Note

• The fastest way to increase your scores is to pay the "Pay at Least" amounts on your credit card above.

PART 3

BUSINESS FINANCE

Pillar 3

Business Credit

Fig. 11 Business Credit

Most people understand personal credit, or they have at least talked about it. But did you know there is another type of credit out there—business credit? You can build business credit just like you can build personal credit, but business credit is ten to a hundred times more powerful. Of course, to build business credit, you must have a business. I am aware that some people reading this may never desire to own or run a business. Statistically, only around 13 percent of the US population owns a business. What I am hoping is that after reading this section, you recognize the power that business credit can bring, and more people are encouraged to follow their dreams of owning their own businesses. It is one of the most effective ways of gaining financial liberty and building real wealth.

If you are a hip-hop music fan (or you simply have ears), you've probably heard Jay-Z: "I'm not a businessman I'm a BUSINESS MAN, now let me handle my business damn" ("Diamonds from Sierra Leone, Carter, 2005). Talking to hundreds of people in the African American community has made me realize not many really understand what he means. The laws of this country were specifically designed so that businesses can take advantage of many benefits that individuals cannot. That is why banks can charge people 27 percent interest on loans but only have to pay out 1 percent. It is why business owners can avoid paying taxes, but it is illegal for individuals to do so. It is also why businesses can enjoy ten to one hundred times the credit that an individual can enjoy.

What Jay-Z is really saying is that he no longer exists as an individual. Instead, he lives his entire life as his business and enjoys all the perks that come with that. His business enjoys tax deductions that he couldn't get as an individual. He has some legal protections that he would not otherwise have as an individual. And, of course, he can get way more with his business credit than with his personal. Jay-Z the man has done well for himself, but Jay-Z the business has done *extremely* well for itself.

So, what is business credit? The simple answer is that business credit is any credit that is secured using your business' tax ID (Employment Identification Number, EIN) number instead of your Social Security number. The process is similar to building personal credit, but you must have a business that is registered with the IRS. Just as there are three major bureaus for personal credit, there are three major bureaus for business credit. They are Dun and Bradstreet, Equifax Business, and Experian Business. By the way, your personal credit score is called your FICO score, and your business credit score is called your Paydex score. Once you have established yourself as a legitimate business, you can begin building and using your business credit. Once again, business credit gives you access to typically ten to one hundred times the financial resources you would normally have access to with personal credit.

Many companies can help you to build your business credit. And just as with personal credit, we suggest you use one to ensure you don't make any missteps that could hurt you or your business. The steps may vary from company to company, but the process is the same for every company that helps you to establish and build business credit.

Phase 1: Business Legitimacy

In this phase you establish yourself as a legitimate business so you can get access to the resources that business credit brings. You will: (a) name your business, (b) register with the desired state, (c) register with the IRS so you can receive your tax ID number, (d) set up business bank accounts, (e) build a website, (f) get a business email address, (g) get a phone number, and (h) get an office space. Let's address each one of those steps in greater detail.

Naming your company seems like a simple and easy step, but a mistake here can cost you in the long run. When naming your business, think of something that allows your business to grow and does not limit you in any way. For example, ABC Enterprises is a great name because it allows you to conduct many types of businesses. Quite often people start businesses selling a particular product or service and then make a change and sell different products or services. For example, Tasha starts a successful networking engineering firm called Nexxus Network Engineering. After three years of successfully running that business, she decides to turn it over to her son and focus her attention on real estate development. She would have to register her new business separate from her first one because the name doesn't work for real estate development. However, if Tasha had named her first company Nexxus Enterprises, she could make that switch very quickly without having to change much documentation. Naming her business Nexxus Enterprises also allows her to create DBAs (doing business as), which can be service- or product--specific and operate under the Nexxus Enterprises umbrella (that is, Nexxus Enterprises DBA Nexxus Network Engineering and Nexxus Real Estate Development).

There are several business structures you can use when registering. These include sole proprietorship, partnership, limited liability partnership (LLP), limited liability company (LLC), S corporation, C corporation, and B corporation. LLCs are extremely popular because they give a greater level of protection than many sole proprietorships but is easier to manage than the corporation structures. We could go in-depth with the differences between them all, but we'll save that for another time. There are many resources online that explain differences in great detail and are available to you free of charge. However, we strongly suggest you understand the differences before setting up your business.

As mentioned previously, you will need to get a tax ID number—also known as an entity identification number (EIN)—from the Internal Revenue Service. To do so you can simply go to the IRS website and file it online. The website is: https://www.irs.gov/businesses/small-businesses-self-employed/apply-for-an-employer-identification-number-ein-online. The steps are self-explanatory, but you may want to consult with someone who has expertise in registering tax IDs before you attempt to do so yourself. There is no cost associated with registering, and once you completed the steps, you can download a copy of the actual tax ID certificate to keep for your records. Note that as of 2021, an individual is allowed to file online for a maximum of two EINs.

When you have registered your business with the state in which you intend to operate, the state will send you the documentation to prove it. Then you can open your business bank accounts. The banking component is a critical one because experience shows that many startup businesses have difficulty determining how to manage their finances. While there is no hard and fast rule for how you should set up your banking and manage your money, here's a simple suggestion that helps you keep track of your revenues and expenses. Open three bank accounts:

> *Bank account 1:* A major bank (for example, Wells Fargo, TD Bank, PNC). A major bank will likely be more accessible than smaller ones. For example, if you receive checks, cash, and money from different sources, you probably want easy access to deposits and withdrawals, and a major bank will give you the best access through more branches and online services.

Bank account 2: A local bank (for example, Penn Community, Fifth Third Savings and Loan, First Trust). Later in the business credit-building process you may want access to business loans. Local banks typically have better lending terms and less-stringent requirements than major banks.

Bank account 3: Credit union (for example, Affinity Federal Credit Union, Freedom Credit Union, Credit Union of New Jersey). Credit unions offer many of the same advantages as local banks. However, credit unions may give you even better terms. We must caution you that many credit unions are not insured by the FDIC. But they may be insured by another governing body. That is a bit riskier than banks, which is why we suggest first opening accounts in major and local banks.

Setting up your bank accounts is important, but how you move money through those bank accounts is as well. Some of the most common mistakes found in small businesses is that the owners often reinvest every dime they make back into the business. They don't take money out of the business for themselves, they don't put away money for business savings, and they don't put aside a portion for taxes. Two years into the business, they find themselves exhausted and ready to quit because they were unable to pay their personal expenses, unable to travel the way they planned, are unprepared to meet the emergencies that the business encounters and are sometimes facing huge tax burdens. The stress of this often leads business owners to abandon the dreams they were once so passionate about. There are no hard and fast rules about money distribution, and you should certainly adjust the percentages suggested below if they don't suit you. These percentages are easy to calculate and give an idea of what order you should set aside your income.

- All your revenue should be deposited into the major bank account. Then immediately remove the first 25 percent to put into your pocket or personal bank account. The idea is to pay yourself first so you can take care of personal expenses and benefit from work you have done. This will help you stay motivated to continue operating the business.

- Move the next 25 percent from the major bank account into a savings account that you maintain at the credit union. Every business is going to have some unforeseen circumstances that require emergency funding. This account will serve as a reserve so that you are prepared for those things. Keep in mind, this money is for emergencies only, such as payroll is short or you have to repair a wall in your office that got damaged. It is also for business emergencies only, not personal emergencies. Those must be taken care of out of your personal emergency fund. This is not for an emergency vacation!

- Move the third 25 percent to the local bank account and use it for reinvestment in the business. All your business expenses will be paid from this 25 percent.

- The final 25 percent should be left in the major bank and used to pay your business taxes. Most small business can wait to pay their taxes annually, but quarterly may better suit you. Either way, having that tax money already set aside can be a big help in the long run.

Once you have established your bank accounts and began moving money into them, it is time to establish yourself as an identifiable business entity to prospective creditors. Some of these next steps will come into play in the latter part of the business credit-building process, but the earlier you put them in place, the more credible you will be as a business entity. Although you have registered the business with the state and the IRS, serious creditors may still have difficulty finding you creditworthy unless they can see evidence of a solid business structure. While the order with which you do the following steps is debatable, their necessity is undeniable.

Build a website. That is where most people will look to see if you are a legitimate business. More important, it is where future creditors will look to determine your legitimacy. Your website doesn't have to be a digital Picasso. It just needs to give the viewer some idea of who you are, what you do, and how to contact you. How detailed you make it is up to you. In today's business climate a website is an essential component of marketing. There are quite a few businesses that primarily operate from social media sites, but these are not substitutes for a website.

Get a business email address. How often have you come across business owners who are using a Gmail email address for business? For example, abccompany@gmail.com. This drives me insane, and I have had major arguments about this. Creditors want to see a "branded" business email address, such as tsmith@abccompany.com. Believe it or not, when creditors are reviewing applications, this can work for you if you have a branded email and against you if you don't. You can use any number of services to obtain a business email address. GoDaddy and Google both allow you to create branded email addresses, and they are relatively inexpensive. We also suggest you purchase enough addresses that everyone on your team can have one.

Get a local phone number and/or an 800 number. Many people use their cell phone numbers as their primary contacts, which is great for a business owner. The difficulty is that cell phone numbers don't usually get registered in the central business phone directories, thus making it difficult for people who are looking for your goods and services to find you in a Google search. Instead, we suggest you get a local phone number and attach it to an 800 number, although that may not be absolutely necessary. You can get those phone numbers from services like RingCentral or Grasshopper. Once you have gotten your number, it works really well if you register it with 411.com. This is the largest business phone directory, and it allows your phone number to appear as a clickable link on a Google search.

Get a commercial space. This is where many businesses try to cut costs and corners, and I completely understand. However, creditors often deny credit when the business owner uses a home-based business address. The thought is that it is easier to walk away from a home-based business and default on business credit than it is if that business has a brick-and-mortar location. You may wonder, though, *what do I do if my business does not require a brick-and-mortar location?* I'm glad you asked that question. The best thing to do is get a virtual mailing address that allows you to receive mail. There are many services that provide this option. The only thing you want to make sure is that your business gets its own suite number or office address, and it is not shared with any other business.

Finally, in this phase obtain a DUNS number. That number is a free business identifier issued by Dun & Bradstreet, the largest business credit organization in the country. Having the DUNS number will not only help you establish your business credit but what you can use in place of your Social Security number on credit applications. You get a DUNS by simply going to the Dun & Bradstreet website and applying for it. Again, a DUNS number is given for free, so you don't have to pay for any of the other services Dun & Bradstreet offers unless you choose to. Once you have received your DUNS number, you can begin building your Paydex score, which as mentioned previously, is Dun & Bradstreet's equivalent of a FICO score. That Paydex score is vital because it allows creditors to track your business credit payment history.

Phase 2: Vendor Credit

Vendor companies often offer credit that will allow you to buy products or services and pay for them later. These vendors will send you the products you order followed by an invoice. Most of them let you pay on what are called "net 30 terms". Net 30 means you have up to thirty days to pay the invoice. There are also companies that have net 60, net 90, and net 120 terms. The number just indicates how many days after the invoice date you have to pay the invoice. The important thing to note about business credit is that your Paydex score is directly tied to when you pay the invoices. The closer you get to the end of the term as far as payment is concerned, the lower your score. In other words, you should pay your invoices as quickly as you can. No more than two weeks after the invoice date is preferable.

The process of ordering and paying for products and services from these companies is called a "payment experience." It takes five payment experiences to establish a Paydex score. You could have one payment experience from five vendors, five payment experiences from one vendor, or any combination of them. The suggestion is that you choose one experience from five vendors. Creditors like to see a variety of vendors as opposed to one because it gives them more confidence in your ability to pay. Think about it. If Rob came to you to borrow money, wouldn't you rather know that he borrowed money from and paid back Sherita, Jamal, Debra, Vicki, and Shaun rather than just Sherita? It would make you more confident that he is going to pay you back.

The great news about vendor credit is that most vendors will extend this credit to you even if it is the first time you are applying for business credit. After all, it is part of their business models. The companies that do this charge a little more for the products you buy than other vendors, but they know you are willing to pay the higher prices in exchange for the credit that they help you build.

Phase 3: Merchant Credit

Merchants are any stores that issue business credit cards and/or business credit lines. These are stores you are familiar with, like Staples, Home Depot, and Lowe's. It makes the most sense that you choose merchants with the products and services you need to run your business. For example, if you are running a home repair business, Lowe's and Home Depot would be great choices. If you are running a hair salon, Target and Sally's Beauty Supply might be best for you.

The key to getting approved is knowing the company's criteria for approval. Before you apply, call the company, and ask them what your business needs to have in place in order for you to have the greatest chance of approval. This is where hiring a company with expertise in helping clients build business credit comes in. They may know that criteria already.

When applying for merchant credit, online applications typically require that you include your Social Security number; it is a required field, which means you must put your number in before you can submit the application. Instead of completing the online application, fill out a paper application, and in the section that asks for your Social Security number, put your DUNS. Now you are getting business credit without giving a personal guarantee. Once your credit lines have been approved, then buy the products and services that you need to run your business. Keep in mind that paying your credit early increases your Paydex score, so keep track of when you purchase. The same rule applies for merchant credit as it does for vendor credit; you need five payment experiences before moving on to the final phase.

Phase 4: Major Lending

Now that you have completed the first three phases—business legitimacy, vendor credit, and merchant credit—it is time to explore your new financial options. If you did the first three phases correctly, your Paydex score should be around 80 to 100, depending on how you paid your bills. Once you have reached that milestone, you can begin applying for credit cards, auto financing, and loans from banks and other lending institutions using your business credit, not your personal credit to secure them. As we said before, credit unions and small banks usually have the more favorable lending terms, so we suggest you start there. However, there are many lending options, and you should explore all that work best for your business.

Now that you have business credit, you no longer have to rely on your personal credit or depleting your savings to start, maintain, and grow your business. Keep in mind the principle called OPM—other people's money. That says in order for you to build true wealth, you should use other people's money to do so. Business credit is the epitome of that concept. You are using the bank's money to build your business instead of using your own. But you still have to pay it back, so be very careful about this. A good rule of thumb is that any credit you use should generate five times the amount in revenue. For example, if you borrow $20K, whatever you use that money for should generate an extra $100K in revenue for your company.

Action

Do you own your own business?

☐ Yes
☐ No

If you said yes to the above question, what is the name of your business?

If you said yes to the above question, what is your Paydex (business credit) score?

PAYDEX SCORE INTERPRETATION

80-100: LOW RISK

50-79: MEDIUM RISK

0-49: HIGH RISK

Paydex Score_____

If you said no to the above question, would you like to own your own business?
- ☐ Yes
- ☐ No

How much credit do you think you will need to start your business?

- ☐ $10K–$50K
- ☐ $50K–$100K
- ☐ $100K–$150K
- ☐ $150K or more

Name three business credit-reporting bureaus.

_____

If you own a business, business credit is essential for growth and expansion. Use the following tables to progress through the process.

Phase 1 is the *business legitimization* phase. This is when you set up your business so creditors view you as a viable credit option. Much of what you do here is going to be useful later in the credit-building process. You want to start early, so you can build relationships that yield positive results later.

Phase 2 is the *vendor accounts* phase. There are several companies that will sell products and services to businesses on credit. They will use terms like "net 30," "net 60," and so on. This means that you get the products or services now and must pay for them within thirty, sixty, or ninety days, and so on. Each payment represents what is called a "payment experience." It is recommended that you have five payment experiences to establish your business credit score (Paydex) before moving on to the next phase. You can have one payment experience from five vendors, or you can have five payment experiences from one vendor. We suggest the former.

Phase 3 is the *merchant credit accounts* phase. Like vendor accounts, some merchants will also sell you products and services on credit. They may do it in the form of business credit cards or business lines of credit. The payment terms are clearly indicated on the applications. When applying, it is important that you do so without surrendering your personal credit history. As with vendor credit, five payment experiences are suggested.

Phase 4 is the *loans and credit lines* phase. All the other phases were really the buildup for this phase. Here you begin applying for credit that gives you the capital to start, run, or expand your business.

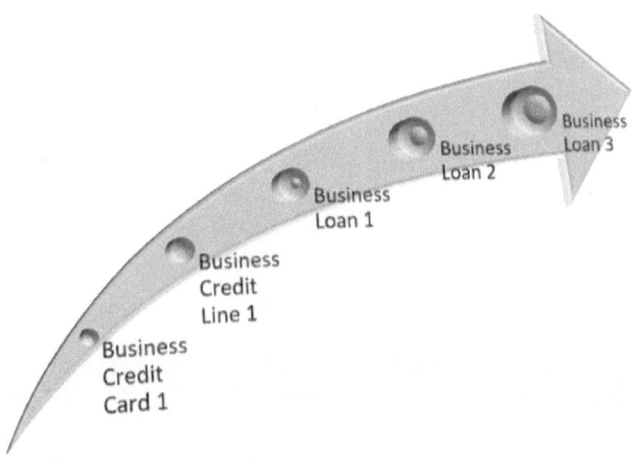

PART 4

ASSETS

Pillar 4

Asset Acquisition

Fig. 12 Asset Acquisition

You have been given a lot of information so far, and I'm certain it must seem overwhelming. You know what they say though: "What's the best way to eat an elephant? One bite at a time." Of course, I'm not suggesting you go kill one of the most precious and majestic animals on earth. This has nothing to do with big game hunting. I'm just using that analogy to explain how you can approach the previous steps. Break each of them down into small pieces. Then do those things one at a time until you have gotten them to work for you. The reason I have you do the other pillars is to get you to this pillar, which is asset acquisition.

Before we get into the how of pillar 4, we should talk a little about the why. As I mentioned previously, when wealthy people have "real talk," they often bring up the OPM principle ... other people's money. They suggest you always use someone else's money to finance your life. However, that principle sometimes requires that you take on debt, and debt is something with which the black community has always had issues. This stems from as far back as the post-slavery era when sharecropping was one of the few options open to blacks after reconstruction failed. The drawback of sharecropping was that many black farmers were given the tools, seeds, and other materials they needed to run their farms on credit, but the repayment rates were so high that they never earned enough to pay their debts. This led to a psychosis in the black community that says debt is bad and living debt-free is good. A debt-free life is in direct contrast to the OPM principle. How can a person live debt-free and still use other people's money? It is not possible.

What many wealth gurus don't emphasize enough is that there is good debt and bad debt, and it is very important to know the difference. Borrowing money to purchase a rental property that is going to yield more in revenue than it incurs in expenses is good debt. For example, if Curtis buys a property that costs him $1,000/month in expenses to maintain it (including every associated expense), but he rents it out for $1,500/month, this is utilizing the good debt principle. Conversely, getting a car loan for an automobile that Curtis does not intend to rent out is considered bad debt. For example, if Curtis gets a car loan for $25,000 and it ultimately costs him $50,000 after he includes interest, the gas he spends over time, the maintenance to keep it running, and any repairs, the only way this could be considered good debt is if Curtis sold that car for $51,000. But that is not typical because a car is a depreciating asset, meaning its value decreases over time. There are some rare occasions when a car increases in value, like if it is a rare vintage automobile or has belonged to someone noteworthy.

More common in the black community is the thought that we have to save up enough cash to buy the asset before we can go out and purchase it. That can be extremely difficult to do. For example, if Curtis wanted to purchase a rental property that costs $50,000, and he saved $1,000 per month to do so, it would take him fifty months, or a little over four years, to save the cash. Chances are that property will not be available when he wants it, or it is going to cost more than $50,000 when he is ready to buy. Also, how many of us can actually save $1,000 per month? That is why the OPM principle is so important. It can give you access to the funds you need to acquire assets long before you can save to get them.

"Asset" is a word that is often used in the world of finance but sometimes misunderstood. To determine if you have an asset, you need only to complete a simple equation:

$$\text{revenue} > \text{expenses} = \text{asset}$$
$$\text{revenue} < \text{expenses} = \text{liability}$$

The trouble in understanding these equations usually lies in the expense component. Many people think that a house is an asset. But if you have a mortgage, maintenance, and recurring bills (expenses), the house is not an asset at present unless you are charging rent and that rent is more than the cost of the mortgage, maintenance, and recurring bills combined. The house could be considered a future asset if when it is sold, it generates more in revenue than it costs in mortgage, maintenance, and recurring bills for the time that it was held. Here is an example of both:

House as an asset
Monthly rent from tenants—$1,500
Monthly mortgage paid out—$750
Monthly maintenance (home repairs)—$250
Monthly recurring bills (water, gas, and so on)—$250
    Total = $250/month asset

House as a liability
Monthly rent from tenants—$1,000
Monthly mortgage paid out—$750

Monthly maintenance (home repairs)—$250
Monthly recurring bills (water, gas, and so on)—$250
Total = $250/month liability

Many people forget about the maintenance and recurring bills, which is why the house isn't a true asset unless the first example is true. This is the case with all assets. If the asset costs you more than you make from it in revenue, it is not an asset.

Before getting into the different types of assets, let's discuss the two types of OPM financing options. Type one is debt financing. Simply put, this means borrowing money from someone and paying it back with interest. If you borrowed the $50,000 to buy that rental property, then you are debt financing it. It may cost you $60,000 in total once you pay back the debt. However, if you make $100,000 either from the sale or the total rental of the property, then it was more than worth it to debt finance. There are many sources of debt financing, including banks, private lenders, friends, and family. Each has its advantages and disadvantages depending on your specific situation. You should, of course, research them all before taking any financing and put yourself in the best situation possible. And always—I mean always—be careful when borrowing money from family and friends. Many families have been torn apart because of money. In fact, didn't Jay-Z rap about shooting his own brother? It was over money.

Type two is called equity financing. This is using someone else's money who will share in the profitability of your asset. For example, someone gave you the $50,000 to buy that rental property in exchange for 25 percent of the profit. Keep in mind that profit means all money left over *after* all expenses have been paid, including the original $50,000. In equity financing the person or institution providing the money recognizes that they are extending money today with the intent of receiving profit in the future. This is a risk to them because, if your business isn't profitable, they don't receive the anticipated returns and, therefore, could lose the original investment. That risk, however, can have enormous rewards and makes it possible for you to have funds that don't have to come out of your pocket.

You get the difference between debt and equity financing now? Good, now we can get into asset acquisition. There are quite a few assets that you can invest in, but understand I am not a licensed financial adviser. The advice I can give is if you are the investor, be sure to consider your level of risk—how much you can afford to invest—and risk tolerance—how comfortable are you with the possibility of losing it. Some people are more conservative than others when it comes to investing. If you are extremely conservative, you may want to examine assets that are low risk. High-risk assets generally yield high rewards. If you are more liberal, this can work in your favor. The important point to note is that acquiring assets can put you narrowly on the path to financial liberty.

This was previously mentioned, but the point should be emphasized that wealthy people measure themselves in net worth rather than income. Net worth is the measure of your assets minus your liabilities. If you are still measuring yourself in income, you are not using wealth principles. People often say they are rich because their job pays them $100k per year in income. However, what happens if they lose that job for whatever reason? Will they still be rich? Not unless they have assets, and even then, those assets may not be working for them the way they want. On the other hand, a wealthy person who has acquired assets that work for them will have many more resources to sustain them in economically uncertain times.

Many people have some common misconceptions about purchasing assets. The most common is that you need a large sum of money to start investing. That couldn't be further from the truth. Here is a way that you can acquire assets by doing something you may already be doing. Many people, including children, teenagers, and adults, like wearing the Jordan brand of sneakers. Authentic Jordans can cost anywhere from $150 to $450 per pair or more. For the sake of this example, though, let's say they cost an average of $150. If Anita buys a pair for $150 and sells them for $175, she has an asset. Of course, she wouldn't want to wear them before she sells them so that they can maintain their value. Why would anyone pay $175 for a sneaker they could pay $150 for? Convenience. It's possible they don't have time to go to the store and get them, or the stores in their neighborhoods don't sell them or have their size, or the pair is a hot release and sell out quickly. There are all sorts of reasons why someone would pay. The $25 profit Anita made from the sale makes those sneakers assets. However, the downside is that she no longer has the sneakers to wear. There is a simple fix. She could buy another pair and sell them for $175. She would keep doing this until the profit she has made from the sales equals the $150 they cost. Now other people have literally paid for her sneakers. Anita could take it one step further and keep selling them until she has made $175 in total profits, and she will have the sneakers to wear herself plus $25 profit. Now she has a true asset.

Assets are neither difficult to acquire nor have to cost thousands of dollars. What is important is that we change our mindset about acquiring them. Assets come in the form of stocks, bonds, mutual funds, real estate, businesses, and so on. But you can also look at your personal car as an asset. Even if you have a car payment, you can still turn your vehicle into an asset. Let's look at the following example:

Car payment—$250/month
Gasoline—$250/month
Maintenance—$250/month
                    Total—$750/month

If you drive Uber or Lyft and make $1,000 per month, you have a $250 per month asset.

You could do the same thing with a bicycle by delivering food for the various food delivery services. You could also turn your wardrobe into an asset. Steven buys clothing from thrift stores and resells them on eBay for enormous profits. He makes sure he goes to thrift stores in affluent neighborhoods, where people often give away unused brand-name clothing and shoes. He may buy those items for $20 or less and sell them on eBay for $300 each. The profit that he gets from the sales of those thrift items is what he uses to purchase the clothes he wears.

All of the things mentioned above are ways that assets can be acquired. What's important to note is that money is not the most difficult barrier to overcome. The discipline to delay the gratification of acquiring assets is much harder. For example, if you choose to buy stock, you may buy it at $5 per share, but it may take two years for that stock to increase in value to $20 per share. In the sneaker example, it could take one year to get enough profit from the sales to pay for your own sneakers, which means you would not get to wear them for twelve months. Delayed gratification, however, is how the wealthy get that way. They understand that if they sacrifice today, they can increase their net worth tomorrow.

An easy example of how to visualize delayed gratification is to think of all assets in terms of cupcakes. If you really like cupcakes and someone said they would give you one cupcake but if you wait until tomorrow, they would give you five cupcakes would you wait? That seems to be a simple choice. However, some would say they really want that one cupcake today and having the other four cupcakes is a bit excessive and almost makes them look greedy. They will pass on the other four and just have the one. Later during the week, they will likely complain about the person who waited and took all five cupcakes and is eating one at the end of the week because that person has a cupcake and they don't. This is how many people view wealth. They hate on these individuals because they believe that having more resources than the majority of the population makes them greedy. However, with five cupcakes you can have one and give four of your family members or friends one each. Now five people each have the same enjoyment as the one who chose to take the cupcake now.

Asset acquisition is, of course, oversimplified here. And by no means do we want you to believe that it's not challenging. The only thing we hope to achieve here is that you understand what assets are, how to acquire them, and how to make them work for you. The most important thing, though, is to begin acquiring them. The sooner you start, the sooner you can accumulate wealth that can last for generations. We strongly believe that you are doing yourself and your family a great service when you build generational wealth.

Action

Once again we revisit the balance sheet. Fill out the sheets below. If you need more space, you can write on another sheet of paper.

Assets			
Savings	$_____		
Stocks/Bonds/ Mutual/CDs	No. of Shares	Cost/Share	Total Value
		$_____	$_____
		$_____	$_____
Totals		$_____	$_____
Real Estate	Down Payment	Cost	Balance
	$_____	$_____	$_____

	$_____	$_____	$_____		
Totals	$_____	$_____	$_____		
Businesses	**Down Payment**	**Cost**			
	$_____	$_____	$_____		
	$_____	$_____	$_____		
Totals	$_____	$_____	$_____		
Liabilities			$_____	$_____	$_____
Credit Cards			$_____		
			$_____		
			$_____		
			$_____		
			$_____		
Total			$_____		
Auto Loans			$_____		
			$_____		
			$_____		
			$_____		
			$_____		
Total			$_____		
Real Estate			$_____		
			$_____		
			$_____		
			$_____		
			$_____		
Total			$_____		
Miscellaneous			$_____		
			$_____		
			$_____		
			$_____		
Total Assets – Total Liabilities = Net Worth $_____					

Update this sheet at least once per month to
see how your net worth increases.

PART 5

FREEDOM

Discipline

The process we use is called the Four Pillars of Financial Liberty (4PFL), but the pillars don't work without two very important principles: discipline and wealth preservation. Webster's Collegiate Dictionary (2017) defines discipline as, "an orderly or prescribed conduct or pattern of behavior." Kevster's dictionary (there is no such thing) defines it as grinding. Many would agree that consistency is the key to success, and consistency definitely requires discipline. On the days when you feel like you have had enough, it will be the discipline that keeps you going.

Let's talk about how discipline shows up in each pillar. In budgeting, discipline can easily be identified. In fact, without it, budgeting is not possible. If Monica sets a monthly budget of $200 for entertainment but lacks the discipline to stick to that budget, then setting the budget was useless. She may still achieve her goals, but it will be extremely difficult and may take considerably longer to do so.

In personal credit, discipline is vital. The lack of discipline has led to the enormous amounts of debt in this country at large and the black community specifically. Take Keith for instance. If he doesn't exercise discipline with his credit cards and increases his use to 80 percent, it could cause his credit scores to drop thirty points or more. Low credit scores lead to higher interest rates, higher payments, and more frequent denials of credit. Over the course of ten years, that lack of discipline could cost him thousands of dollars. On the flip side, having discipline could earn him tens of thousands of dollars in assets.

Business credit discipline is the ability to continue in the process. When building business credit, the laws and policies are much more forgiving than with personal credit. High credit utilization does not lower your score like it does with personal credit. However, it typically takes approximately twelve months or more for a business to establish business credit. And the longer it takes to put all the pieces in place, the longer it will take to access the tens of thousands of dollars that business credit can afford you.

In the pillar asset acquisition, discipline is evident in how you obtain assets. One of the reasons Denzel Washington has been able to have a successful and enduring career is because he maintains the discipline to choose his movies carefully. He never takes on a role that may typecast him in any way. In asset acquisition, the same principle applies. Don't pursue an opportunity that doesn't yield a true asset. There are countless examples of people who have been taken by get-rich-quick scams. Having the discipline to do thorough research could have prevented some of them. This is not an attack on anyone's character, and there have certainly been many examples of savvy people who have still been conned. I am simply saying you can avoid some of the issues with discipline.

If discipline is an important principle to all four pillars, then certainly wealth preservation is the other. Everything you have read so far has led you here. You have created a budget and established savings, learned to manage your personal credit, established a business and leveraged business credit, and invested your money in true assets. Now it's time to preserve your wealth. One of the most important lessons ever taught is that it is extremely difficult to pass wealth along through generations if it is not protected. Let's discuss some of the ways to preserve wealth.

One of the most essential protections of wealth is health insurance. These two things go hand in hand. I guess that is why they rhyme—health and wealth. To explain how health affects wealth, let's look at a fictional example. Donald is a self-employed commercial contractor who is doing pretty well for himself. Donald has six employees working for him and takes home $130K/year in salary. Donald has managed to save approximately $67K over the course of the last three years, which he will use for personal emergencies. Donald's monthly expenses total approximately $6,300 including $987 in student loans. Donald is single, lives alone, and does not have any children. As a result, he has not seen the need to get an adequate health insurance policy outside the required minimum coverage for self-employed individuals.

One day while working in one of his commercial buildings Donald tears his rotator cuff and breaks several ribs in an unfortunate accident. Because he is the person who secured the contract to work on the building and the state requires he be on the jobsite every day with his crew, he is deemed vital to the project. Donald decides that he needs emergency surgery so he can get back to work as soon as possible. Between the ride to the emergency room, the surgery, and the rehabilitation, the total cost of his hospitalization is $96K. His health insurance will only cover $16K of those costs. Donald quickly burns through his $67K in savings and now has to finance the rest of the bills, which totals $13K. In addition, he has to take out a loan to pay some of his employees and his personal expenses for the time he is out of work, leaving him $40K in debt.

As you should be able to tell from the example, Donald has spent the substantial assets he had, his savings account, and now has liabilities of

$40K. His lack of coverage cost him $107K ($67K loss in savings + $40K in new liabilities). For $350/month, he could have had a policy that would have covered all those bills and kept him from blowing through his savings. With his insurance premiums costing him $350/month, it would take him twenty-five years of payments to equal the $107K it cost him ($107K ÷ $350/month ÷ 12 months/year).

Many people refuse to get insurance or adequate coverage because they say it costs too much. We suggest replacing the term "cost" with "investment." Don't look at insurance as a cost; instead, look at it as investing in your wealth protection. If someone said, "Give me $38K, and I'll give you back $100K in return on your investment," would you do it? Of course. They would have to show you how that was possible, but if it were a legitimate investment, you would jump at it. If you consider that health care costs the average human $11K per year over one's lifetime, and adequate health insurance costs them an average of $4,200 per year, that is pretty much the same investment. You are investing in a product that protects your earliest asset ... you.

Like health insurance, disability insurance is also necessary for wealth protection. A disability is always a possibility, but it doesn't have to be a scary thought. A disability could be something as simple as a broken foot. What if Derek is working on his construction site and breaks his ankle, causing him not to be able to work for four months? He does not have the ability to make money for those four months, which means he may have to dip into his savings, live off of his credit cards, or even sell some of his stock. Do you see how this minor injury could reduce his wealth? In addition, I'm sure we have all seen how ridiculous medical bills can be. An ambulance ride alone can cost $500. If you include the X-rays, anesthesia, and the actual surgery to repair the ankle, you could be talking $12K when it's all said and done. With disability insurance, Derek can offset the costs of his medical bills and preserve his wealth.

If you think that health insurance and disability insurance are scary to talk about, just wait until I introduce this next topic. A health issue or a disability issue is only a *possibility* in your life. People can go their entire lives without having a major health or disability issue that causes them to blow their wealth. However, there is one inevitability no person big or small, short, or tall can escape ... death. That's right, every person on this planet is going to die someday. Yes, I know it is an extremely morbid thought. The problem with most people is they don't feel comfortable discussing it, and they definitely don't plan for it like they should.

Wouldn't it be a shame if Lashira spent fifteen years building a successful manufacturing company that gave her $500K in assets, but she passed away prematurely and left behind $600K in debt? Now her children and other family members may have to take on that debt. Or at least they wouldn't get access to the $500K in assets. This is where life insurance kicks in. If I told you that you could invest $100K over the next twenty years and that investment would yield $1M, would you make that investment? Of course, that assumes I could prove to you that your investment was legit. Well, that is what life insurance does for you. If Lashira had a $1M policy at the time of death, her children could pay that $600K in debt and still have $400K in assets.

Life insurance is a great way to pass wealth on to other generations. What you must know is that you should have the right amount of coverage in the right type of policy for the right amount of time. A properly structured life insurance policy is an asset in itself. I am not an insurance expert, so I suggest you find one and discuss your options. In fact, it would be a good idea to find several because some of them will tell you that term life is better than whole life, and some will tell you the exact opposite. Get differing opinions and invest in the one that gives you the maximum amount of coverage you should have given your life circumstances. It is up to you to do that research, but it really is not up to you to go without having life insurance. This is a must!

Did those last three sections get you scared and depressed? That was not my intention. It was simply to help you understand how important those things are to maintaining your wealth. Since you will be worth billions in the next few years, I want to make sure you can keep it. This final topic should bring you back around, though, so don't worry.

You've heard of that brown paper bag under your mattress money. That is how many people keep cash hidden from those who may be looking to take it. Not a bad idea if you're hiding a few thousand, but can you really keep one million under your mattress? Besides making the bed uncomfortable, you know someone is bound to find it. And if you have a fire in that room, it could be lost forever. Furthermore, if the IRS finds out and you haven't paid taxes on it (which is why many people are hiding it there in the first place), you could be looking at some serious issues.

So how do wealthy people use the same technique to protect their money ... tax sheltering. When people hear this, they often think of movies in which they see rich people sending their money to the Cayman Islands so the IRS can't touch it. While this is certainly a thing, I am not talking about that. I am talking about using the tax laws of this country to your advantage. There are hundreds of laws written for businesses and individuals that allow people to protect their wealth. The best suggestion is to find a good tax accountant who keeps current with these laws and have him or her explain to you how you can make those laws work for you.

Don't forget it is against the law not to pay taxes, and you know the old saying, "All I have to do is stay black and die." Well, that's not all you have to do. You also have to pay taxes. The goal, however, is to pay as little as you can, so you can keep as much as you can and pass it on.

Action

Get a health insurance policy. Once you have it, fill in this table.

Name of Company	Policy #	Primary-Care Physician	

Get disability insurance. Once you have it, fill in this table.

Name of Company	Policy #		

Get disability insurance. Once you have it, fill in this table.

Name of Company	Policy #	Face Value Amount	Monthly Premium

This book is certainly not the only resource that discusses wealth principles. However, black wealth seems to be much more challenging to achieve in the United States. I have found that it typically takes longer and is more difficult for African Americans to achieve a net worth of $100K or more than it is for other Americans. That doesn't mean it is impossible, and we have countless examples of African Americans who have been able to achieve net incomes that are even greater. My aim is to provide you with some simple steps you can use to achieve that goal.

One important point we want to mention, though, is that nothing is achievable without action. There are quite a few people on this planet who say, "Knowledge is power." While that is true, rewriting the statement and saying, "The application of knowledge is power," may be more accurate. For example, let's say you learned how to change a flat tire on your car by watching someone else do it on their car, and you took great notes while you were watching. You now have the knowledge to change a flat tire. However, if your car gets a flat tire while you are driving on the highway in the rain and don't get out and change it, that knowledge did not have the power to get you where you needed to go. At least not by you anyway. Now some could argue the point that you could use the knowledge to instruct someone else to change your tire, but it is the action that gets the tire changed, not the knowledge.

I believe so heavily in the statement that the application of knowledge is power that we included in each section of this book the action items that go with each pillar. Most human beings are only able to do a few things at once before they become overwhelmed, so we encourage you to commit to one pillar for a specified period. You could decide to do one pillar per year, one pillar per six months, or one pillar per month. Whatever you decide, we recommend that you not try to do them all at once. They may come as huge adjustments to your lifestyle, and your discomfort may make you want to quit. Decide what works for you, and just make sure you are doing something. You can also combine these pillars with other information you have learned to help you achieve the wealth you desire. Never forget, however, that you can only achieve a goal by starting the process.

Four Pillars of Financial Liberty
4PFL

Financial Liberty

Discipline

Budgeting Strategy

Personal Credit

Business Credit

Asset Acquisition

Income

BIBLIOGRAPHY

Chris Colmar (December 28, 2020). Richest Neighborhoods in Philadelphia, PA For 2020. Retrieved from: Richest Neighborhoods In Philadelphia, PA For 2020 Richest Neighborhoods In Philadelphia, PA For 2020 (homesnacks.com).

R. Scobel (n.d). How many vacations do wealthy Americans take per year? Blog comment. Retrieved from: How Many Vacations Do Wealthy American's Take Per Year? - Pursuitist

Merriam-Webster's Dictionary (11th ed.) (2003). Discipline. Springfield, MA.

Carter, S. West, K. "Diamonds From Sierra Leone." Late Registration. Def Jam, 2005

Hello family, friends, and associates. I'm Kevin Lewis, the CEO and principal consultant at Premisien. Our team has counseled many people on the issues of financial liberty and wealth building. What we have found is that many people want to be in better financial positions but haven't found the right motivation. We decided that we would give them a push and do our part to increase financial liberty in America.

Our team has come up with what we call the "Prosperity Pledge." We are challenging everyone to make a video reciting the four statements of our pledge. We then would like you to act on those statements. We have teamed up with the Youth Financial Literacy Foundation (http://yflfoundation.org/) to give people an incentive.

Here are the instructions for your pledge:

- Make a video with the words "PROSPERITY PLEDGE" on the bottom and post that video to all your social media pages. Please say the following in the video:

Premisien Prosperity Pledge

I pledge to have at least three months of living expenses in savings.
I pledge to have a personal credit score of at least 720.
I pledge to have a business credit score (Paydex) of at least 80 (for business owners).
I pledge to acquire at least one asset every year.

- Tag at least one of your connections, the one(s) who is(are) most likely to take the pledge in the video.
- Go to our business page (https://www.facebook.com/Premisien-278708699237340/) and post a picture or video of one of your goals (for example, your dream house, your dream car, your dream vacation) to help people understand why you are taking the pledge.
- If you choose not to participate in the challenge, we ask that you donate at least a dollar to the Youth Financial Literacy Foundation, http://yflfoundation.org/.

Thank you for taking this pledge. We believe this is a giant step in the direction of eliminating the wealth gap in America!

www.ingramcontent.com/pod-product-compliance
Lightning Source LLC
Chambersburg PA
CBHW021453210526
45463CB00002B/766